MI$ERLY MOMS

Living On One Income In A Two Income Economy

SECOND EDITION

Jonni McCoy

FULL QUART PRESS

Values Worth Preserving

MISERLY MOMS:
Living On One Income
In A Two Income Economy

Copyright ©1996 by Jonni McCoy

Recipe on page 221 (Liquid Soap) is provided with permission of
Deborah Tukua, editor of *Coming Home* magazine.

ISBN 1-888306-14-9

Cover Design & Book Layout
by Mark & Wendy Dinsmore

For information contact:

Full Quart Press
PO Box 254
Elkton, MD 21922-0254
Tel. (888) 669-4693

NOTE FROM THE PUBLISHER AND THE AUTHOR:

*This book is based upon personal experience, interviews and research
by the author. Although much effort was made to ensure that all
information in the book is safe and accurate, this book is sold with the
understanding that the author and publisher assume no responsibility for oversights, discrepancies, or inaccuracies. This book is not
intended to replace medical, financial, legal, or other professional
advice. Readers are reminded to use their own good judgment before
applying any ideas found within this book.*

Printed in the United States of America.

*I would like to dedicate this book
to my dear husband, Beau.
Without his tangible and emotional support,
I would never have written a book.
He gave me many hours of writing time
by watching the kids, doing extra housework
and attempting to cook for us.
His suggestions were always on target.
He also never failed in his belief that
I could write something of value.
He always has believed in me.
It is through that encouragement
that I have become the woman of God
that I am today.*

ACKNOWLEDGMENTS

This book would not be possible without the ideas, suggestions, and advice of many friends and family. Their generous assistance and ideas were so very helpful. In the first edition of this book I listed those who helped me. This edition had so many helpers that I cannot list them all; but I want to give a special thanks to four people who contributed a great deal.

To my mom, Joan Stivers, who not only helped in editing, but also in laying the foundation that lead to this wisdom. To my dad, Jerrold Stivers, for his many good ideas and financial training. And to my dear friends Denise Weigel and Donna Salinas whose ears I bent endlessly. To the many others who generously shared your ideas, please know that I always will remember your kindness.

CONTENTS

INTRODUCTION

WHY I WROTE THIS BOOK

Our family lives in one of the most expensive cities in America. Most people (even lower income) spend half of their income just to pay the high rent/mortgages. Consequently, most families in our area need both parents working, just to get by. We were one of those families. According to statistics, my husband and I were a middle income family with my job providing half of our income. We enjoyed some of the yuppie amenities such as a nanny (part-time), Kona coffee flown in from Hawaii, and weekends at a bed and breakfast on the coast.

After a few years, I wanted to stay home full-time to raise our family. But we couldn't live in this area on half of our income. At least that's what we believed. We decided to move somewhere that cost less to live, that my husband could commute from. We were ready to move, but things changed at the last minute. I already had quit my job when we had decided not to move. So, here we were living on half of our income in an expensive area.

Our choices were for me to go back to work or to somehow reduce our expenses. I felt strongly about staying at home with my family; I didn't want to go back to work. I began to research how to make our money go farther. This opened my eyes to the hidden costs in the way we live, and I questioned whether some people could even afford to be working.

When we had calculated what our loss of income would do to our budget, we didn't realize how many hidden costs would also disappear once I quit work. Working is very expensive. Given the cost of daycare, taxes, gasoline and parking costs, convenience foods (since we were often too tired to cook after work), lunches out, office clothes, and all of the other amenities associated with working, not much of our salaries is used at home. Some financial experts have calculated the cost of working as $9–16 per hour. I was stunned! This meant that if I earned $10 per hour, I was only seeing $1 for every hour that I worked.

I looked at ways to bring in some income while staying at home, but I was inspired by the challenge of reducing our budget instead of trying to increase our salary. Therefore, I am not filling this book with ideas on how to make money at home. Many other books have done a fine job of that (I've listed a few of these books in the resource chapter for those interested in pursuing this option).

Many books have been written on how to be thrifty. Some are theoretical in their approach, filled with interviews and statistics. Some are focused on a specific area to save, such as credit cards or groceries. Others try to be broad, but are too extreme, cutting in every aspect of life, whether it is cost-effective or not.

I look at saving money as a means to an end. It is a job I perform in order to pay for my staying at home. I don't do the things that I share in this book just for fun. I enjoy my luxuries if I can afford them. Some people enjoy being frugal as a hobby. I, however, must be convinced of the cost return to me before I do something. For example, I find little profit in reusing envelopes or dryer lint. Those activities may save 1¢. This would not be a good use of my time. If you only have a little time to invest in saving, it might as well be put to use in the most effective place.

I believe in finding where your time spent being frugal will give you the best cash return. This is why the book is organized as it is—from the greatest area of savings to the least. Groceries are the first and largest topic that I discuss, because it is where families can save the most. We were able to save $250 per month in this one area. I discuss other topics in which we also were able to achieve a significant cost savings. When added together with the loss of working expenses (the cost of working), we made a large dent in what we spent—adding up to what some people might be earning at a job.

Some people already have thought of the ideas in this book. Especially those with parents or grandparents who lived through the depression and have passed on their frugal tips. There is much "lost wisdom" from those who knew how to make what was necessary and live without the unnecessary. But many have explained that they needed help being creative in the cost-cutting areas of life. It is for these people that

I decided to write this book. My desire is to get your creative ideas in motion, so you can start thinking of ways to save in your home.

Your spouse doesn't have to be earning a high wage for you to live on one income. I know several families (including my own) who willingly live on less than half of what the average family in their area earns.

I have put all of the principles in this book into practice. We still live in the same home as we did when I quit my job. We have added a member to our family. We go on vacations. We buy nice things for our kids and ourselves.

These principles really make a difference.

What do you have to lose?

IF I CAN DO IT, YOU CAN DO IT

You might think that it comes naturally for me to be organized, self-disciplined and to spend some extra time doing shopping and baking. This isn't true. It didn't come naturally for me. I share my background, not out of vanity, but to show you that anyone can learn to live frugally.

The first thing you should know is that I am not tight. It is not in my nature. I do what I have to in order to reach a goal. I can (and do) return to my luxuries in a snap when I can afford them. Some people are frugal because they never knew any other way. I knew what the good life was, but was able to learn to live frugally when I needed to.

Until the age of eight, I lived in a Northern California suburb, Walnut Creek. My family lived an average middle-class life with a three-bedroom house, a dog, and simple vacations to Yosemite and the beach. Then life changed radically. My dad accepted a job with an American organization in Pakistan, and then later moved to Nigeria. When the plane landed overseas, life would never be the same. We suddenly had five servants and a three-story house with bedrooms the size of most living rooms. We traveled around the world several times in the six years that we lived overseas. We returned to the United States when I was 15, buying a three-bedroom house in Silicon Valley (south of San Francisco).

I share this to help you understand that I knew what good things were, but was able to learn to do without them. Since I was used to the convenience of having food made and work done for me by others, learning to apply myself to the art of being thrifty was new to me. The skills that I have acquired and share in this book were necessary to reach my financial goal of staying at home with my kids. It didn't all come to me at once. I started with one idea, then added another one later. Eventually, I started to see a difference. Even if you only apply one or two ideas that are in this book, you will help your budget.

So, if I can do it, you can do it.

The Eleven Miserly Guidelines

T HE ART OF BEING MISERLY interested me when I needed to find a creative alternative to working. When I quit my well-paying job, we had planned to move to a cheaper area. Shortly after deciding not to move, I had become pregnant. I already had decided to stay home instead of returning to work, but this door was now firmly shut (Who's going to hire a lady with a growing belly?). Since I was not going to bring in money by working, I decided to attack the problem from the other side—reduce what money went out of the house.

The first thing I did was look at those items in our budget that were not fixed. This was any expense that fluctuated (such as food, gasoline, clothes, utilities). My next plan was to chip away at them. I started with the highest of these bills—food. The eleven guidelines were originally notes that I kept for reducing my grocery bill—the highest expense after our mortgage. They were notes I kept in a binder for myself. I never intended to share them with anyone. But with the encouragement of friends, I wrote some articles, then the first edition of Miserly Moms, then this. With this second edition, I have added other areas to save in, aside from groceries. As I learned more and expanded my horizons beyond the grocery store, I added more notes to my notebook. Even though the eleven guidelines are mainly for food, the general principles can be applied to other areas of your home.

By doing some rethinking on how I shopped and cooked, I immediately lowered our food bill from $100 per week to $65 per week. That was a savings of $140 in that first month. As I learned more ways to save and applied them, the less I spent. These ways to save eventually became my eleven guidelines. I have been able to lower our food bill to $40 per week on many occasions. This of course can only happen if all 11 guidelines are being applied faithfully. We average between $60–65 per week on groceries, mainly because I buy a few convenience items. Four years later and one more family member, we are still able to achieve this goal of $40 per week if we work at it.

If I compare this savings to the value of a part-time job, my budget cuts have proved to be more profitable. A 20 hour per week job paying $5 per hour (less taxes, baby-sitting, and other expenses) would provide only $80 per month. That's only $1 per hour profit. I "earned" more than that applying my guidelines. If you believe that these ideas may be too much work, divide what you saved that week by the hours spent doing the shopping and cooking. It should come to $5–8 dollars per hour (expense and tax free!).

I have found many helpful resources to reduce our budget deficit. The most helpful have been cookbooks that contain recipes on how to do things yourself—cereals, jams, etc. The ones written in the 30s and the late 1800s are my favorite. They are full of recipes for homemade versions of things that we think can only be purchased ready made. Some of my favorites are listed in the Resource chapter at the back of the book.

With ideas gathered from these "classics," I have formed some guidelines for grocery buying that make high savings possible, such as my occasional $40 per week grocery bill. Below I have outlined the general guidelines. More specific suggestions follow in the chapters.

Some of these ideas may seem far-fetched; take what you like, and leave the rest. For those just starting out on the odyssey of reduced spending, all eleven ideas may be overwhelming. After I spoke at a seminar, a woman came to me "in distress". She thought she had to apply all eleven ideas immediately. As I told her: take one step at a time. Pick one idea and apply it. When it becomes comfortable, apply another one. Even if you only choose to try a few of the ideas, you will save. The more ideas, the greater the savings.

THE ELEVEN
MI$ERLY GUIDELINES

1 *Don't confuse frugality with depriving yourself.*

2 *Give up things that provide the least value.*

3 *Keep track (written down) of food prices.*

4 *Don't buy everything at the same store.*

5 *Buy in bulk wherever possible.*

6 *Make (and grow) your own wherever possible.*

7 *Eliminate convenience foods.*

8 *Cut back on meats and poultry.*

9 *Waste nothing.*

10 *Institute a soup and bread night once per week.*

11 *Cook several meals at once and freeze them.*

GUIDELINE ONE:
Don't Confuse Frugality With Depriving Yourself

T HIS IS THE MOST IMPORTANT aspect of being successful at saving money. If I think I am being cheap when I try to save money, I never will stick to my guidelines. My underlying attitude is more important than any guideline I try to follow. It is essential to my success.

If any money-saving activity makes you feel cheap or tight, then you will abandon your saving ways, thinking that this is how all saving ways are going to make you feel. That is not the price we need to pay to reach our goals. I don't need to feel tight and cheap in order to stay home with my kids. There are other ways to save money and keep my dignity. Many people think the two cannot be linked.

I am not tight by nature. I know many people who love to be thrifty, but not because they need to. Rather, it is a hobby or fetish to them. Many frugal newsletters advocate dumpster diving and reusing envelopes and dryer lint. I always have to ask myself, "Why?" Are these things worth the time? What do they pay you, in terms of reaching any goals that you have? A reused envelope saves you a penny. Dumpster diving may find things you can use, but did you need those things? Even if you did, what toxic elements were you exposed to while saving those few dollars?

While I was working, many women I knew wanted to be at home with the kids, but most believed that the price would be too high to stay home. These were career women who were used to good clothes, nice vacations, eating out regularly, extra cash for impulse items, etc. They believed that in order to live without their income, they would have to resort to dumpster diving, and a cheap lifestyle. So most remained working. I am living proof that there is a balance between these two.

I look at eating leftovers and eating out less often as ways to reach my financial goals, instead of as something that I have to do. We still go on vacations, but less extravagantly. When I grumble about cutting corners, I remind myself of my financial goal. Mine is to stay home with my kids. Yours might be a vacation, or a purchase. I remind myself that the temporary luxury of a pre-packaged meal, a shopping spree, or a meal out is less important than reaching that goal.

Money and class are not synonymous. You can be classy and thrifty at the same time. I'm not saying that it's always easy. I enjoy nice things and going places impulsively. Always planning for everything is hard. On those days when it is hard for me to remain frugal, I need some help to stay on track. I have devised some incentive boosters to help me when I am feeling uninspired. Here are my two favorites.

- *Divide the savings of one week by the hours spent saving it (shopping, cooking). Calculate the amount "earned" per hour. For example, last week I saved $60, and it took me 7 hours to do it. That means I made $8.50 per hour profit—tax free, no sitters, no expenses.*

- *Have a visual reminder. Put the budgeted grocery money in an envelope. You can see the leftover money when the week is over. That's yours to spend where you want to.*

Hang on to your attitude about why you are saving, and the rest of the guidelines will be easier to hang on to.

GUIDELINE TWO:
Remove Little
Wasters of Your Money

W HEN I KEPT TRACK of everything that I spent over a month's time, I was surprised at how many times I had squandered money. This is an activity that I recommend to anyone who is serious about saving money.

If you have a computer, get a software program that will keep track of all check categories as you enter them into the check register. We use a program called *Quicken* by Intuit. It reconciles our checkbook. While we do that, it shows us our spending habits, by asking for a category for every check you write (no fair getting cash for everything). You can then run reports by category and see where and how much was spent. This is very enlightening. You can also create a budget. You can track investments and plan for retirement. *Quicken* is not the only program that offers these services. Among others, there is Microsoft's *Money,* Kiplinger's *Simply Money,* and MECA's *Managing Your Money.* No matter which program you use, you will save yourself much time and effort in maintaining your family budget.

Those little trips to Target and lunches out at McDonald's will keep you from reaching your financial goals. It is amazing how much of a drain they are on the budget. When I feel like dropping into the golden arches or going to Target, I remind myself that those trips make things unattainable that are higher in priority on my list. Those trivial buys here and there can wipe out all that you have saved. One lunch per week at a fast food restaurant costs $35 per month (one adult and two kids). I could apply that towards a bill or vacation fund.

I have friends who "need" to shop for recreation and who work full-time to pay for it. I wonder if the recreation is to ease the stress of work, or is the work to pay for the recreation? In either case, the drains need to be plugged if any progress is to be made in reaching the financial goals.

This guideline should come as a natural by-product of the previous guideline. More specifically, many of the little wasters of our money are done to make ourselves feel good. We must reprogram our thinking about money. It should never be used to make ourselves feel good, or to be a measure of someone's love for us. Money should be looked at as a tool. It's there to get you where you need to go.

In order to make things work, I have to make a budget and stick to it. Anything that I want to do that isn't budgeted for has to wait until I save enough for it. The importance of a budget cannot be understated. If you need help creating a budget or learning to live within one, I have listed several good books on budgeting in the Resource section at the end of this book. You can't go wrong with books written by Larry Burkett or Ron Blue on budgeting or getting out of financial debt.

For those that cannot control themselves, I suggest that you put the budget into cash envelopes if you have to. Have a separate envelope for each area in the budget. Take the money out of the bank and keep it in the envelopes. When the envelope is empty, you will have to wait until next month. If keeping lots of cash around is a worry, only take it out of the bank weekly and keep it in a safe place at home.

When we lost half of our income, it was a matter of survival for the first year. I had to stick to a tight budget or we would go under. I did whatever was necessary in order to remain frugal. If I had weak knees at the sight of a "sale" sign, then I would turn my head when I was near department stores. If impulse shopping at the grocery store would overcome me, then I would only shop once a month to avoid those overwhelming temptations. When I have shared these ideas with people, some look shocked or say, "Oh, that's just too drastic." Nothing is too drastic if it's important to you.

GUIDELINE THREE: Keep Track of Food Prices

WHEN I STARTED my adventure of squeezing even more money from each dollar spent, I thought I knew what most things cost. Someone suggested that I write prices down, and see if I knew as much as I thought. This was the most educational activity that I could ever do. Prices are NOT about the same everywhere.

I started to keep track of prices on foods in my local stores. At first I started writing down the regular retail price of things that I commonly used at each of the stores. Then I added the best sale price for those items at the same store. By adding the best sale, I created a goal for myself. For every item, I always included the unit price (ounce, pound) so I had an easy comparison. This is very important as package sizes vary. Many companies are reducing the size of their containers instead of increasing their prices (i.e. tuna cans used to be 6 1/2 ounces, but are now 6 1/4 ounces).

I keep this list in a small notebook (I used a pocket calendar) that easily fits in my purse. I created columns for food types and then rows for the price and unit of measure information. Below is a sample of what's in my notebook.

COLD BOXED CEREAL

Store Name	Brand	Retail Price	Best Sale	Best Unit Cost
Lucky's	LadyLee	$2.29	$1.99/20 oz.	10¢/oz.
Safeway	Cheerios	$2.89	$1.99/20 oz.	10¢/oz.
PriceCostco	Cheerios	$5.89/40 oz.		14¢/oz.
PriceCostco	Quaker Granola	$2.29/16 oz.		13¢/oz.
Homemade	granola	99¢/16 oz.		6¢/oz.

By breaking prices down, I can take a quick glance as to where an item is the least expensive. And surprisingly (to many), it wasn't cheaper at the warehouse store.

From this list, I began creating goals for myself. I aim never to buy an item for more than the best sale price that I have seen. This becomes my target. For those of you just starting out, I have included a copy of my target prices. This is meant to help you get started in your shopping. If we don't have a target to aim for, we settle for what's available.

PRICE GOALS

Food Item	Pay No More Than	Average Price
Drink mixes (make 1 qt.)	25¢ per package	50¢
Frozen concentrate drink	99¢ per 12 oz. can	$1.69
Ground meat;		
beef	$1 per lb.	$2.39
turkey	69¢ per lb.	$1.69
steaks, roasts	$1.50 per lb.	$1.69+
Chicken (parts or whole)	39¢ per lb.	$1.69
Chicken (boneless, skinless)		
thigh	$1.58 per lb.	$2.89
breast	$2.99 per lb.	$4.89
Seafood (whole fish)	$1 per lb.	$4.00+
Tuna	50¢ per 6 1/4 oz. can	69¢
Dry cereal	$1.69 per box	$3.89
Granola	$1 per lb.	$2.50/lb.
Butter	99¢ per lb.	$1.49/lb.
Margarine	50¢ per lb.	79¢/lb.
Toilet Paper (off brand)	59¢ pkg. of 4 /15¢ per roll	$1.29

Food Item	Pay No More Than	Average Price
Toilet Paper (Charmin)	99¢ pkg. of 4 /25¢ per roll	$1.89+
Paper Towel	50¢ per roll	89¢
Fruit (apples, oranges, pears, etc.)	59¢ per lb.	69¢
Potatoes	10¢ per lb.	25¢ per lb.
Oil	4.5¢ per oz.	8¢ per oz
Dish Detergent/Cascade	4¢ per oz.	6¢ per oz.
Cheese	$1.69 per lb.	$2.39 per lb.
Peanut Butter	8.3¢ per oz.	12¢ per oz.

I set target prices for other areas of my life as well. I know what I can get something for and I avoid paying much more for it. For example, I know that a homemade dinner for four people usually costs me $3. This is easy to achieve.

Knowing and having this goal keeps me from ordering an $18 pizza or spending $35 for dinner at a restaurant. You can do the same with other areas such as clothing or books. I have included my cost goals for meals to help you start setting goals for yourself.

COST GOALS

Snacks

KEY TO SAVING IN THIS AREA: Buy only one per week—when it's gone, they have to wait!

- *Make homemade instead of store bought (popcorn, popcorn balls, pumpkin bread, cinnamon toast, cookies)*
- *Eat fruit and veggies with dips (homemade)*
- *Visit day-old bread outlets for cookies, chips and crackers*

Price Goals: 5–10¢ per person/per snack

Breakfast

KEY TO SAVING IN THIS AREA:
Avoid dry cereals and prepackaged mixes.

- *Make homemade alternatives (muffins, pancakes from scratch, French toast, eggs, hot cereal)*

   Price Goals: 25¢ per person/per meal

Lunch

KEY TO SAVING IN THIS AREA: Avoid convenient mixes and pre-made foods

- *Avoid fast food and other restaurants*
- *Make homemade sandwiches with lunch meat on sale*
- *Make homemade soups*
- *Put homemade lemonade or fruit juice in a thermos—avoid juice boxes*
- *Use leftovers from other meals*

   Price Goals: 50¢ per person/per meal

NOTES: Feeding a family on a tight budget is tough, and everyone will have to sacrifice. The kids will have to eat leftovers (so will you) in their lunches. Invest in a lunch box size freezer pack so that the kids can take perishable items to school (tuna sandwich, lunch meat, leftovers). Also invest in a small thermos for soups and one for juices.

Dinner

KEY TO SAVING IN THIS AREA: Avoid convenient mixes and pre-made foods.

- *Avoid fast food and other restaurants*
- *Stretch the meat with vegetables and beans*

   PRICE GOALS:
   Budget meal for 4–$1 total
   Average meal for 4–$3 total
   Special meal (seafood, roast, nice occasion) for 4–$5

GUIDELINE FOUR: Don't Buy Everything At The Same Store

O F THE 11 GUIDELINES, I believe #4 ("Don't buy everything at the same store") has been the greatest source of savings for me. Although planning for and shopping at several stores is the biggest time expenditure in the "job" of being miserly, it provides the biggest payoff. It can save you up to 50% of your grocery bill.

No one store has the lowest price—not even the warehouse clubs. As I learn more about the art of being miserly, my bills keep dropping. There are two main stages to shopping: planning and deciding where to buy. If you do these two stages while rolling through the grocery aisles, you cannot save anything. You must become aware of who sells what, and what it costs. You can incorporate coupons and rebates, but they must be secondary to where and what you decide to buy. Below is an explanation of how I do my planning and shopping.

PLANNING

The worst mistake shoppers make is to show up at the grocery store and just buy what they think they'll need that week. Even if you choose to do all of your shopping in one store, just having a list will reduce your spending. Planning is essential to your saving success. Most people think of planning as picking their menus for the week, making a list and buying those things at the nearest store. I want to challenge you to rethink your planning and shopping process.

Instead of taking an arbitrary menu plan and shopping around it, plan the menu and lists around the grocery sales. One friend of mine saved $30 the first time she switched her planning to my suggestion. She didn't apply any of the other tips in the book. She just planned the menu around the sale items, instead of picking recipes arbitrarily.

The best way to prepare for a shopping trip is to read sale flyers from your local grocery stores. They are usually in the food section of the newspaper. Many stores send them directly to your home. Then build a menu plan around these sale items. I save even more if my menus are based on low-cost recipes found in my miserly cookbooks. After I make my menus based on sale items, I make grocery lists for each store.

SHOPPING

Once my planning is done, I go to each store and buy only those things I have listed. I first visit the more expensive stores and buy their good sale items on my list. Don't impulse buy. Don't look up and down the aisles for what's available. It's important to remember that those stores with the greatest sale prices (or "loss leaders") and double or triple coupons tend to have higher prices on everything else. Their sale prices are great, but their other items tend to be 20% higher than most stores. They have to recover their losses somewhere. This is why it is important to buy only their sale items. I go to two or three stores this way, getting the sale items I need for my menus. I finish at the store that I find to be cheapest overall and buy their sale items and the rest of my grocery list.

Many people might say, "Why spend all that time going from store to store? A few cents saved at one store won't pay for the gas of hopping around." It's not just "a few cents" being saved, as you'll quickly realize after one week's worth of shopping. You might lose your savings if you drove long distances to the two or three stores that you chose. All of the stores should be within 10 miles of your home, so that gas isn't an issue. I figure that I use $2–$3 in gas each week to save $30–$40 in groceries.

I usually do all the shopping in one afternoon, as it is easier to finish all at once. Take a few days if it works better for you. Or, send your hubby to one of the stores with a precise list. Some weeks I find only two or three items on sale that interest me at the "secondary" stores. When this happens, I skip those stores that week. It has to pay off to go to the extra stores.

Beware of the great sale! Sometimes a store announces a big-name item at a great price, but they only offer one of its products at that price. For example, a store recently advertised Oscar Mayer hot dogs at $1.50. The average store price is $2.49. But only one of Oscar Mayer's three types of hot dogs was offered at this price. The other two were over-priced at $3.99 each. Watch the fine print. There are certain stores that do this type of advertising regularly. If the store that you frequent is always out of the sale item, drop them from your shopping routine. Many purchase a limited stock of the sale item, then hope that you will purchase a more expensive version instead. Ask for a rain check. Some stores won't give one until the last day of the sale. So shop there on the last day of their sale and get what's in stock, and the rest next week with the rain check.

To add even more savings, watch for free grocery coupons in the mailers. Some stores put out a flyer every few weeks for free food items or super savings with purchases. Here you can save even more on the food bill. One week I got a 10 lb. bag of potatoes and two cans of tuna for free. This converted into soup, a casserole and potato salad. That's three meals for which I didn't pay!

Another source of savings are the store coupon books mailed to homes. These prices are great and worth stocking up on the items you normally use. These coupons have to be used carefully also. Another reminder is to only buy what you need. The good deals tempt us to buy even though we don't need it. Buy the sale items. The rest of the store's prices are higher in order to recover the losses on these coupons.

You aren't alone in reaching your goal. There are many companies that exist to help the Miserly Mom. There are the warehouse club stores, the grocery outlets, the supermarkets, day old bread stores, and specialty outlet stores. They can make your job easier, and hopefully help you to stay on track. You must know how and when to use them. Let's look at each type of store.

Warehouse Clubs

The most well-known companies are the warehouse club stores, such as PriceCostco or Sam's. These club stores can save you money, but only on certain things. I see people buying everything they need at these stores, thinking items are cheaper. You must know your prices before you can shop there. Because this type of store is so popular yet tricky to use, I have set aside an entire chapter (chapter 14) to discuss their use.

Supermarket Warehouses

There are also supermarket warehouses that offer bulk foods and minimal services (such as no baggers) to cut costs. In our area, we have Pak'n'Save, and Food 4 Less. These stores carry a more limited variety of name brands than a regular grocery store does, but do have good prices on their store brand items. The only items that I have had trouble with are meats and fish (poor quality) and open bins of bulk foods (people put odd things in them).

Outlet Stores

There are also outlet stores that provide clothing, food, or specialty items. These stores usually are listed by their company name (e.g. Oshkosh, Nike, Wonder, Hostess, Entenmann's, Oroweat, etc.). These are great places to find good bargains. The clothing outlets usually are not cheaper than a department store sale, but their clearance racks are great. The bread stores have half-price loaves of bread and other baked goods. Many have a "cheap" day when things are a dime a piece.

Then there are general outlet stores that carry a variety of goods. In our area, we have:

- *TRADER JOE'S which sells food items of their own brand as well as imported items*
     Good Buys: fish, breads, cereals, vitamins, dairy

- *CANNED FOOD GROCERY OUTLET which sells surplus, outdated, discontinued or dented items at good prices*
  Good Buys: all items are cheaply priced

- *SMART AND FINAL which sells paper products and deli foods*
  Good Buys: paper products, but know your prices

- *COST PLUS IMPORTS which sells imported items, coffee, candy and small toys very cheaply*
  Good Buys: gift items, coffee, candy

- *DOLLAR STORES which have good deals on food and household items. I have seen large salad dressings, liquid drain opener, cold medication all for 99 cents*
  Good Buys: all items are cheaply priced

Visit these stores and compare their prices to those you have written down from your local stores. They may be worth including in your shopping routine.

COUPONS AND REBATES

Coupons can help you keep costs down, but only if used carefully. I don't use them very often. With a coupon, I am tempted to buy something that I normally would not buy–just because I have a coupon. When I am tempted by a coupon for an item that is not on my grocery list, I ask myself three questions: 1) do I need it? 2) can I buy it cheaper in another brand? 3) can I make it cheaper? I have also noticed that coupons usually are for a convenience food that I can make myself or do without. Rarely do you see meat, bread, or milk have a coupon.

It's important to compare prices with the coupon to the price of the same item in an off-brand without a coupon. The name-brand item plus a coupon may still cost more than the off-brand item at regular price. And the off brand items are not inferior in most cases. Actually, many off-brand items are name brand items bought at a discount (surplus) and then relabeled. It may seem great to turn in a bunch of coupons and get $20 taken off of your $100 purchase, but wouldn't it be better to buy $60 of groceries without any coupons?

Coupons are great for saving money, and even greater if a store offers double coupons. But, again beware of this trap. Most stores offering double or triple coupons have higher prices on most of their groceries. They have to recover the cost of those extra coupons somewhere. I usually just purchase the items that I have good coupons for, and take the rest of my list somewhere else.

Places to find "good" coupons are the Sunday newspapers, local library coupon exchange boxes, and local coupon clubs. Ask neighbors or friends for their Sunday paper if they aren't going to use the coupons. If your library doesn't have an exchange box, ask if you can start one.

Another good way to get coupons of high value is to write a note of appreciation (or complaint) to the manufacturer of a product you use. They usually send several valuable coupons for my trouble.

Once you have some coupons, keep them in a small portable filing system. I file by food category (snack, breakfast, side dish, vegetable, dessert, household items, baby). Some people file alphabetically or by expiration date. Whatever the method, keep them with you when you shop.

Take advantage of the coupon books mailed out by certain stores. These stores hope to draw you in with your entire week's grocery list. If you just buy the coupon items, you can save big. Remember to take the rest of your list to the cheapest store nearby. With these coupon books, I stock up on the cereals, soups, and other items I will use during the next four to six weeks. That's about when items will go on sale again somewhere else. Each time I use a coupon book, I get $30–$40 taken off at the register.

You can maximize your savings if you use a manufacturer's coupon at the same time as you use a store coupon. It is legal to do this since one is issued by the store and the other by the food manufacturer.

Rebates can be great, especially if matched with a sale and coupons. You have heard stories of how someone only spent $20 for $120 worth of groceries by combining coupons, sales and rebates. It can be done, but this usually is a rare event. There are avid rebate fans who spend up to 20 hours per week reading rebate newsletters, clipping, mailing, and filing grocery receipts and proof of purchase seals. I can't help but repeat myself—would I buy these things anyway? It's cheaper not to buy them at all.

Some people are opposed to using coupons under any circumstances. Their reasons vary. The most common complaint is that coupons increase the price of food since the manufacturer must recover the costs somewhere. This is a valid concern. But boycotting coupons will not drive the prices back down again. A good example of this is a recent marketing strategy by Proctor and Gamble. Many people have written asking them to stop issuing coupons and lower their prices instead. They did stop issuing coupons, but (as of this writing) they have not lowered any prices. Many manufacturers won't drop coupons for that reason. They are concerned if they drop coupons and lower prices, the retail stores will absorb the lower cost and not pass it on to you. They feel a coupon is the only way to pass the savings directly to you.

Other reasons for avoiding coupons involve the purpose of coupons. Some think coupons are for first-time buyers only, issued to convince you to try a product. To clarify the intent and purpose of coupons, I wrote to three of the largest food manufacturers (General Mills, Kellogg's, and Nabisco) and asked their intent when coupons are issued. They said coupons are for both newcomers as well as repeat buyers. This makes sense since coupons are put inside food packages. Only a repeat buyer could use that coupon. The food manufacturers consider coupons an advertising medium. If coupons were outlawed, they would take that cost and convert it into another form of advertising.

Overall, I do not encourage an excessive emphasis on coupons. There are coupon clubs and subscriber services for coupons. I think you eventually lose with these. The real savings is following the lowest price—whether that is a sale or an off-brand. Occasionally that lowest price may be the use of a coupon plus a sale. Then it is to your advantage. But I think we have been lead to believe there is a pot of gold to be found, if we use enough coupons. Remember they, along with several other things, are tools to help you reach your savings goal.

CO-OPS

Another source for food at low cost is a co-op. They can provide organic (and other) products at a lower cost than most local stores. Items that you might buy in a health food store are usually much cheaper through a co-op. Knowing prices is essential. I have found a few items in stores to be cheaper.

Most co-ops are formed when some friends want to get foods wholesale and cheaper than what's available. They find a cooperative company that will allow new members in that area (many areas are closed due to retail store pressure of the competition). Someone orders and receives the shipment, divides the orders and handles the money. Many groups also hold meetings and seminars on nutritional cooking.

Many co-ops have a mail order system in which you receive a quarterly catalog and send in your request. These types of businesses usually sell in large quantities, such as a case of cereal boxes or potato chips. This sort of buying is good for people who consume a great deal of certain items, or who can split a case with someone. Beware of the traps of being in a co-op. Some groups require a minimum dollar amount purchase every month. This can be binding if you don't need to buy or don't have any money that month. I also have found that I tend to over buy when I have been in a co-op. Even though an item was a great price, I didn't need 12 of them. I also tended to buy things that I normally wouldn't–just because it was wholesome and a great deal. But did I really need it? Could I make it myself?

If there isn't a co-op near you, form one yourself. Check your local phone book for cooperatives. Call a local university and ask them for a listing of local co-ops in the area. Ask friends at church or work—word of mouth is a great form of news. If none of these provide help, write to the National Cooperative Business Association, 1401 New York Ave NW, Suite 1100, Washington D.C. 20005 or call them at (202) 638-6222. They will give you the regional headquarters of cooperatives near you.

Another great source of general information on all types of cooperatives is *The Whole Co-op Catalog* offered by Twin Pines Cooperative Foundation. They offer books and videos on how to start any type of co-op (food, worker, housing, agricultural, baby-sitting). They also explain the legal and financial aspects of starting one, and have directories of co-ops across the nation. You can call them at (510) 538-0454 or write to them at 1442A Walnut Street, Suite 415, Berkeley, CA 94709 to receive a catalog.

EXCHANGING SERVICES

Our culture is relearning the skill of exchanging services. This was the original form of business transaction for America. The early settlers bought and sold goods by offering something they had made in exchange–such as homemade cheese for a handmade woolen item. This form of business is still active. Many do it casually by finding something they can offer and asking others if they would consider exchanging services. A friend wanted to join a local pool for the summer, but couldn't afford it. So she offered to do a service for them in exchange. She painted their changing rooms in exchange for her family's membership. Other friends exchange lawn care, hair care, wedding services, auto repair, ironing, sewing, etc.

For those with more elaborate needs or those who live where there are limited resources, there are national exchange groups. The groups list what you are interested in obtaining and offering. They usually charge a high annual fee for this service. Local churches sometimes have a listing of services that is free and more than enough for most.

I have never used any formal service for my exchange needs. I arrange the exchange by asking. As my mother always said, "You'll never know the answer until you ask."

LOCAL FARMS

Another source of savings is local farms and ranches. If you live near one, ask about discounts on eggs, milk, or poultry. Look for roadside stands near farms. Many homeowners who are avid gardeners set up a stand in their front yard to sell their extra produce. Write to the

Chamber of Commerce for a list of any farms that allow you to pick your own produce.

If you live near a dairy, purchase milk and cheese. If the trip is far, stock up. Both milk and cheese freeze fine. Eggs freeze well, but to avoid cracked eggs, try mixing them into your recipe first, then freeze before cooking. If you live near a chicken farm and can get a good deal on eggs, here are some tips on how to tell a good egg from a bad egg:

To tell if an egg is fresh, place it in a pan of cold water.

- *If the egg lies on its side, it is fresh.*
- *If it tilts, it is 3–4 days old.*
- *If it stands upright, it is probably 10 days old (use these for baking).*
- *If the egg floats to the top, it is old and should not be used.*

To add to my savings on eggs, I purchase two types of eggs. Our local egg ranch sells regular grade AA and "checks and dirties." The checks and dirties are eggs with imperfections in the shell. These eggs have a higher risk of contamination and shouldn't be eaten unless completely and thoroughly cooked, such as in baking. These imperfect eggs cost 69 cents per dozen and save money since I bake frequently.

GUIDELINE 5:
Buy In Bulk
Wherever Possible

BUYING IN BULK SEEMS LOGICAL, but there are basics to learn in this savings lifestyle. There are two types of bulk buying: large container sizes or large quantities of small container sizes. The best savings is earned with both types of bulk buying.

The large quantity form of buying is when I stock up on a good sale. For example, this would be buying a box of paper towels on sale for 29¢ each. Or buying many loaves of bread during my monthly visit to the day–old bread store. I figure what I will use during one month and buy that amount. I say one month because that is approximately when it will go on sale somewhere else. If you can stock up for two months you are better off.

Buying in large container sizes saves money because you are reducing the packaging and handling required by the manufacturer. It is really worth it to buy in bulk and deal with the minor inconvenience of repackaging the food into meal size bags or finding some storage space. Starting may be difficult because of the cost involved. Eat very cheaply the first week, and use that savings to make your first bulk buy. Each week will be easier.

Two good examples of this savings are hamburger and chicken. Compare the prices of the different packaging types;

Hamburger (lean)	
individual 1 pound packages	$2.39/lb.
10 lb. chubs	88¢/lb.

Chicken breasts (boneless/skinless)	
individual packages	$4.59/lb.
warehouse clubs/bulk	$1.58/lb.

Ask among friends and neighbors to see if anyone works with a meat distribution company to buy meat at wholesale. If this is unavailable, ask your butcher or meat department how much ground beef or turkey you would have to buy in order to get a discount. It might be 40 pounds or more. Don't laugh—the price is worth it. The lean hamburger that would cost more than $2 per pound will now be 99¢ per lb. The ground turkey that is usually $1.39 per lb. will now be 69¢ per lb.

Believe it or not, you can handle all of that meat at one time. Form some meat into meatballs and freeze them in baggies (each baggie is a meal portion); make a huge kettle of chili and freeze in meal size portions; and slice the rest into one or two pound chunks and freeze individually for later use. You can ask friends if they want to join with you. I buy my meat this way. My friend has to buy 70 pounds of ground beef to obtain a good price. We split it among four families and each of us prepares and freezes our portion. I don't have an extra freezer and I still can do it with ease.

Another benefit of bulk buying is that it helps avoid running out of something, and rushing to the store to pay full price.

Some of you say you can't buy in bulk because you don't have the space. If I can do it, you can do it. I live in a small townhouse and have no storage space. I have figured out how to use the little space that I have. I use old bookshelves in the garage for a pantry. I don't want an extra freezer, so I went to the local hardware store and bought a plastic coated wire rack and put it in my tiny freezer above the refrigerator. The added shelf doubled the amount of useable freezer space. If you are motivated, you will be amazed what you can find.

CONTAINERS

One woman asked what I store bulk food purchases in. As I stated above, I have learned to use every space available. I know of people who store canned goods under beds or in hallway cupboards. I haven't done that yet.

When it comes to storing things, I certainly don't want to spend my money on expensive plastic boxes. For freezer space, I store my meals and food in zippered plastic bags. When filled with a meal, they are only 1/2 inch thick. I am able to stack several of them on top of each other. Once frozen, they can be turned sideways and stacked like records. If I used plastic boxes, I would not be able to fit my meals in the little freezer.

The cost of these bags is minimal. I pay between one and two cents per bag by watching sales and using a coupon at the same time. I use 30 per month for main meals (that's about 50 cents per month). I can wash many of them for reuse. It would take many bags to make an extra freezer worth it.

After World War II, people started demanding convenience foods. With this change, we have lost some of the wisdom of home-made foods and storage that our grandparents learned. People who went through the depression let nothing go to waste. Every thing was put to a new use. One of the things saved were containers that foods came in. Even the flour sacks were used to make dresses (the material was a soft cotton with a floral print). Here are some of the things we can glean from their experiences:

- *save all jars that you bought something in (mayonnaise, syrup, etc). Reuse them for your homemade syrups, chocolate sauces, salad dressings, etc.*
- *save cardboard oatmeal boxes as storage containers for dry goods (your homemade granola, bulk items bought from bins, or even small toys).*
- *save cereal boxes for magazine holders (cut the side off, diagonally).*
- *ship cookies to friends in Pringles cans. They reduce breakage.*

- *wash out plastic mustard squeeze bottles and fill with home-made colored frosting for cake and cookie decorating*
- *reuse margarine tubs for food storage. The largest sizes available (usually 5 lb.) are large enough to store food for one meal. The smaller containers are good for leftovers, lunches and side dishes*
- *many people reuse resealable freezer bags by washing carefully, and then checking for leaks.*
- *if you make your own baking mixes, save the large dry laundry detergent buckets. Wash out WELL before use.*
- *check the $1 stores periodically. I have found good plastic boxes with lids for $1 each.*

GUIDELINE SIX:
Make Your Own Wherever Possible

G UIDELINE #6 ("Make your own wherever possible") has been one of the more exciting of the 11 guidelines, as it is a never ending exploration with rewards in discovery.

Most people believe they need to buy everything that they need; but it wasn't long ago that we made everything that we needed. People even made their own baking powder. Recipes for just about everything that you use can be found in some cookbook. The older the book, the better. Garage sales and libraries are a great source for these cookbooks. One of my favorite newer cookbooks is the More-With-Less Cookbook written by Doris Longacre. This is full of recipes for simple homemade alternatives to common grocery items such as cereals, soaps, breads, etc.

Depending on your source for homemade alternatives, making your own can save you more than pocket change. I don't cook from scratch to get a homey feeling. I do it if it saves money, or if it will be more nutritious. There are a few things that are cheaper to buy than make, but not many.

To get the most from my time in the kitchen, I looked at my areas of spending and attacked the highest expenditure. I reviewed four weeks worth of grocery receipts and categorized my expenditures by food type (dairy, breakfast, meat, vegetables, snacks). I picked the area of the highest spending and went to work, creatively replacing them with homemade alternatives. Below are the areas that I began making instead of buying. They are in order, starting with the area in which we spent the most, ending with the area in which we spent the least.

BREAKFAST

My highest spending area was breakfast foods. We spent $40 per month on this one meal. Most homes rely on prepackaged cereal for this meal. We did too. This has become a very profitable business for the manufacturers. The average box of cereal costs $3.50–$4.00. Many families eat two or three boxes per week. That's $28–$48 per month just for cereal. This is a worthy target for the miserly arrow.

My first move was to introduce alternatives to cereal two to three times per week. I don't slave in the kitchen every morning. When I make muffins, hot cereal or pancakes, I make a large batch and freeze them for other meals. Pop them in the toaster oven or microwave for a meal. Don't use prepackaged baking mixes. You will lose your savings on them. Baking from scratch takes about the same amount of time as using a baking mix. If you're addicted to these, make your own baking mix. Many cookbooks have a master baking mix recipe, and many uses for it.

I then experimented with recipes for cereal. I found one for grape nuts, several for granola, and some for mueslix style cereal. All were delicious and only a fraction of the cost of store bought versions (remember that the manufacturers have to pay for all that glitzy advertising). I occasionally buy cold boxed cereal when it is a good sale combined with a coupons. This way I only pay $1–$1.50 for a box of cereal. With these changes, I reduced my breakfast spending to $12–20 per month. That's half!

Sample of Cost Comparisons:

Breakfast food	name brand	homemade
granola (1 lb.)	$2.89	$1
pancake syrup (24 oz.)	$3.19	11¢
frozen microwave pancakes (12)	$2.47	34¢

SNACK FOODS AND DRINKS

My next highest area of spending was snack foods. This area includes chips, fruit leather, candy, popsicles, ice cream and soft drinks. My first move was to try to introduce fresh fruit or a homemade treat whenever a snack was needed. If this is considered "boring" by your troops, try homemade fruit leather (see recipe in Some Great Recipes). Candy and chips can be replaced by homemade cookies or homemade granola bars. Popsicles or pudding pops can be made cheaply and easily with drink mixes, yogurt or pudding. Soda can be replaced by generic versions of Kool-Aid® or other drink mixes. When frozen concentrated juices go on sale for 89¢ each, we buy several. We still need to control how much of these are used up in a week. If we don't, we tend to drink up in a week what was bought to last a month. One way to "ration" the good drinks is to only allow one cup of the juice mix at meal time, and water after that, if thirsty. Another is to only allow water at mealtime, and juice after the food is finished. This way they don't fill up on the drinks and skimp on the food.

In the chart below, I have compared drinks by their cost per quart (using sale prices at local grocery stores). The average household consumes 16 quarts of soft drinks per month (two soda bottles at two liter size per week). If we compare costs over one month for each of these, the savings is very noticeable:

Beverage	Monthly Cost	Unit Cost
Soda (sale)	$8.00/mo.	(50¢/qt)
Kool-Aid	$4.00/mo.	(12¢/qt)
Generic mix (Kool-Aid style)	80¢/mo.	(5¢/qt)
Gatorade	$6.40/mo.	(40¢/qt)

For a special snack, we make a fruit drink called a smoothie. We put some fruit in a blender (strawberries, peaches, bananas, kiwi, orange, or whatever we have on hand) and add some liquid (apple juice or milk) and blend until smooth. For a thicker texture, add ice or frozen fruit, replace the milk with yogurt and blend. It's refreshing, healthy, yummy and inexpensive (the gourmet shops sell these for $3.50 each).

Another snack that we frequently make are cookies. We enjoy making them together (and eating them together). Most people buy their cookies. I have heard many people talking in stores, saying that you can't make it any cheaper than the packaged cookies, especially when they are on sale. I often wondered if it was really true. So I took out my calculator (again), and figured the following cost for about two dozen chocolate chip cookies:

Chocolate Chip Cookies (2 dozen)	Total Cost	Cost Each
packaged cookies on sale	$2.60	11¢
homemade	$1.50	6¢

The most expensive ingredient is the chocolate chips, which I buy when on sale for 99¢ per bag. Other types of cookies are less expensive, such as oatmeal or snickerdoodles. To save on time, I make a double or triple batch of cookie dough. I divide the dough into balls the size of a baseball and freeze each ball. When it's baking time, I thaw one ball and bake the cookies. This way my cookies are always fresh when wanted. For my favorite cookie tips, see Chapter 13, Some Great Recipes.

MEATS

Another high area of spending for many families is meat. I attack this area three ways; buy in bulk, shop warehouse clubs, and replace it with nutritious alternatives.

A few years ago, I read about a woman who had a target price for meat that was $1 per pound. I laughed when I read this, and wondered how I could ever share that goal. Then I began to watch ads. Hamburger occasionally goes on sale for 99¢/lb. (in bulk packaging). Buy a few chubs and slice them into one pound sections and freeze them. When you need a pound, pull one out. Then I saw ground turkey go on sale for 79¢/lb. Scan the sale flyers each week. I have seen pork roast at 68¢/lb., Tri-Tip at $1.50/lb.

For leaner meat, buy a roast on sale and have it ground. Or buy the higher fat ground meat on a good sale, and drain and rinse it to lower the fat. Even though it cooks down, it is still a better deal, pound for pound, than full priced lean meat. You also can go in with a few friends and buy the higher-grade meats in bulk from your butcher or meat department at a good discount.

Hot dogs are a meat product, and can be creatively included in the meal plan. The good brands go on sale for $1 per package (which is a pound). The off brands go on sale for 69¢/lb. To lower fat, buy the lower fat hot dogs when on sale.

At Thanksgiving, many stores offer a lower price on turkeys during the few days before that fattening Thursday. I usually can buy a turkey for 29¢ per pound. Stock up with as many as your freezer can handle. On Thanksgiving, you can bake more than one if the pans will fit in the oven. It does not change the amount of cooking time, nor require more energy than one bird. I try to buy as large a bird as I can fit in my oven. I then have leftovers for a week or more at very little cost or effort. After we eat our Thanksgiving meal, I cut the meat off of the bone and place in bags in meal size portions and put them in the freezer. I serve turkey sandwiches or turkey fillets with the best cuts. As the week progresses, I serve the smaller pieces in stir-fry or creole-type dishes. When I get down to the bone, I make soup with it. Nothing goes to waste. Here are some turkey buying and cooking tips to assist you:

- *Plan on one pound of turkey for each person you are feeding. This does not allow for leftovers, however.*
- *A tom is the male turkey and is usually tougher (but larger). A hen is the female, and is usually smaller and more tender.*
- *To thaw a turkey in the refrigerator, plan ahead. It takes about 24 hours for every 5 pounds of turkey to thaw.*
- *To thaw a bird in the sink, cover with cold water and allow approximately 12 hours for large birds and approximately 5 hours for smaller ones. Remember to change the water often, keeping it cold.*
- *Many cookbooks recommend roasting turkeys breast side up. I prefer to roast my birds breast side down. This allows the juices to run down into the breast, making the meat more tender and juicy.*
- *Loosely cover the top of the bird with foil. This keeps the bird from browning too much and drying out.*

- *Don't keep opening the oven to peek at the bird. You are letting heat out each time, and therefore lengthening the baking time.*
- *For a gourmet touch, rub the skin with half of an orange. Do this close to the end of the roasting or it will burn.*

Another way we beat the high cost of meat was by increasing vegetables, grains, legumes and beans like we are suppose to. This also will lower your fat intake. By using the healthy alternative of rice and bean recipes, it costs less than $1 to feed a family of 4. Rice on sale for 25¢/lb. and beans at 33¢/lb. are nutritious and cheap! I have even found several rice and bean recipes that my picky eaters like. Other ideas are stir-fry, egg and rice casseroles, and potato-based dishes.

Here is a price comparison chart of meat alternatives

- *fish fillets for 4 = $6*
- *steak dinner for 4 = $4–$5*
- *hamburger dinner for 4 = $3*
- *stir-fry dinner for 4 = $2.50*
- *rice and beans for 4 = $1.50.*

PRODUCE

The last high spending area that I noticed was produce (vegetables and fruit). This is not an area that you want to skimp on, but there are ways to reduce the costs. Supermarkets make 30% of their overall profit from their produce section. Once I learned this, I knew there had to be cheaper ways to buy fresh produce.

The first way to save the most in the area of produce is to grow your own. If you have yard space that isn't used much, make it work for you (instead of you working for it by mowing, weeding, etc.). I have a friend who converted her lawn into a huge vegetable garden. She doesn't buy much of her produce. When you grow your own, the vegetables cost about 1¢ each. For more information on how to set up a productive garden for little money, see Chapter 15 on Stretch the Season.

The next best thing I did was take advantage of the farmers' markets. The prices are great! Much of the produce is organic as well as very fresh. Most of the items are allowed to vine-ripen, making them more nutritious. Go at the end of the day and get even better savings. Many farmers don't want to take anything back home with them and are willing to sell cheaply. If you are able to can or freeze, buy extra vegetables and fruit. You'll have plenty of produce on hand, and you'll be able to beat the high off-season prices at the supermarkets. Below is a list of what's commonly found "in season" at a farmer's market. Since things are cheaper when they are in season, plan your menus around these things and reduce the cost of your recipes.

Seasonal Produce Chart

Summer

grapes	avocado
lettuce	zucchini
tomatoes	peaches
plums	

Fall

apples	pumpkins
winter squash	broccoli
oranges	

Winter

broccoli	oranges
acorn squash	

Spring

berries	asparagus
bananas	plums

All Year

potatoes	carrots
celery	

If you can't get to a farmer's market, the next best thing is to stock up on fresh or frozen vegetables on sale. I have seen 12 ounce bags on sale regularly for 50¢. One local grocery chain has an annual 10-cent sale on produce. I stock up on whatever is being sold. I freeze them for future use. This is a great way to get your 5-a-day (nutritional guidelines recommend at least five servings of fruits and vegetables per day).

Some people believe that we must eat fresh produce to obtain the right nutrients. In many cases frozen vegetables can be as healthy as the fresh ones. The only exception to this might be if you grow your own vegetables or you buy organic produce. Produce from supermarkets and produce stands are not as full of nutrients as we hope. First, they have been picked one to three weeks before they ripen, so they have less nutrients than a vine-ripened equivalent. They have been washed and bathed in water mist for 1–2 weeks at the stores to look appealing, which can cause nutrients to leach out. The saddest part is that they have been hybrid in order to look a certain way, and many of the nutrients have been bred out of them. All of this leads back to why a frozen vegetable is no worse than a "fresh" one in the stores. It actually might have more nutrients since it hasn't been sitting around a store for a week or more. They are fast frozen and bagged without being cooked, or ingredients added.

The last and least desirable way to save on produce is to buy canned fruits and vegetables. We don't do this too often, since the canned produce has been cooked and salted, leaving less nutrients than fresh produce. But occasionally it can be a welcome help. I have found that canned vegetables and fruits can sometimes be cheaper than fresh or frozen versions. This can really help your budget if used once in awhile.

Don't forget that fruit and vegetable juices can help us reach our 5-a-day goal. I find these helpful in the winter months when there is less variety of fresh produce available. Fruit juice in the morning and a mixed vegetable juice as a snack are very healthy.

Cooking Tip: A good way to cook vegetables is in the microwave, with either no water or a teaspoon added. All of the nutrients stay in the vegetable, and they retain a good texture.

Comparison of Vegetable Servings Per Pound

Vegetable	Fresh	Frozen	Canned
beans, green	5–6	4–5	3–4
broccoli	3–4	5	3–4
carrots	4–5	3–4	3–4
celery	4–5	3–4	
potatoes	4	3	3–4
spinach	4	3–4	2–3
tomatoes	5	4–5	3–4
cabbage	4–5	3–4	
dry beans	10–11		
most fruit	3–4	3–4	2–3

SPECIALTY ITEMS

With the latest health craze being lowfat and low cholesterol foods, we sometimes think we have to buy these items in order to eat healthy. We need to keep it in perspective. (We also must remember that because something is fat free doesn't always mean it's good for you.) The marketing folks at the food manufacturers know this too. Have you noticed the relabeling on many foods? Hershey's Chocolate Syrup now claims to be fat free. It always has been. Again, all we need to do is learn to cook lowfat. Here are some tips I have learned to make lowfat treats.

Fat Substitute Chart

To lower the fat content in	Replace oil with equal amounts of
cakes, cookies and breads	applesauce
chocolate cake, cookie, brownies	pureed prunes (baby food works well)
sauces and dressings	nonfat yogurt
mayonnaise or sour cream	nonfat yogurt

LUNCHES

Many folks struggle with how to provide a healthy lunch for the kids that can travel in a lunch box. Since I homeschool, I cook lunches for our kids and save a great deal this way. I reheat leftovers or can serve something warm and inexpensive. Whenever I need to pack a lunch, I try one of the following ideas:

Main Dish:

- *tuna fish sandwich*
- *egg salad*
- *ants on a log (celery stick with peanut butter and raisins on top)*
- *bagels and cream cheese*
- *cheese and crackers*
- *lunch meat-when-on-sale sandwich (bologna, ham, turkey)*
- *peanut butter and jelly sandwich*
- *soup in a small thermos with crackers or cornbread*
- *cold pasta salad with whatever they like in it (olives, cheese chunks, artichoke hearts on sale, celery chunks, tofu pieces)*
- *leftovers*
- *black bean sandwich spread on whole wheat bread*
- *tortilla rolled up with shredded carrot and a turkey slice*

Invest in a small freezer pack that can keep any perishable dish cold.

LEFTOVER TIP: If you made enough at dinner time to have some leftovers, but the group ate everything that you made, try this tip. After the meal is made, but before you serve dinner, take the part you think should be the leftover amount and set it aside. What they don't see they won't miss.

Snacks:

- *homemade granola bars*
- *muffins*
- *homemade cookies*
- *carrot or celery sticks*
- *popcorn*

- *homemade pudding, gelatin or rice pudding*
- *fruit*
- *applesauce*

The key is to put them in your own containers and not buy the prepackaged individual serving sizes.

Drinks:

Invest in a small thermos and fill it with juices bought on sale or in bulk, homemade lemonade or milk. Avoid the prepackaged juice boxes or cans. They cost twice as much as filling a thermos.

Some people have commented that the menu I serve at lunch is high in fat. Often you can replace the same item for a lowfat version. For example, buy chicken or turkey hot dogs instead of full beef, or buy the more expensive fat free ones if you can. For macaroni and cheese, replace the milk with nonfat milk and the butter with yogurt. For bagel and cream cheese, buy fat-free cream cheese. Peanut butter is high in fat, but also high in protein. You don't need too much to meet a person's protein needs. The all-natural peanut butters have no added oil. For the tuna and egg salad, you can replace the mayonnaise with nonfat mayonnaise or nonfat yogurt. Disguising the taste with relish is helpful. Ham lunch meat is usually as low in fat as turkey, so watch for sales or bulk prices at warehouse clubs. They are often cheaper than turkey.

Staying within budget and keeping it healthy at lunch takes the same planning and forethought as other meals. You can do it.

GUIDELINE SEVEN: Eliminate Convenience Foods

C ONVENIENCE FOODS have eaten up (no pun intended) many of my grocery dollars in the past. I have shopped when hungry, looked at those yummy looking packages that say, "you can eat me now—without the fuss," and taken them home. I have smelled and tasted the samples available during peak shopping hours — and bought the item.

Convenience foods are just that—convenient. And you are going to pay someone for that convenience. Sometimes we pay more than we think. Making your own meals and snacks from scratch can make a big dent in your food bill. In my price studies, this is what I found about convenience food pricing:

- *A restaurant meal costs 6 times more than if made from scratch.*

- *A frozen meal will cost 4 times more than if made from scratch.*

- *A prepackaged mix costs 3 times more than if you made it from scratch.*

- *Pre-cut foods (ready salads, sliced carrots, shredded cheese) costs 2 times more than if you cut them yourself.*

One of my favorite examples of this is the microwave french fries in the freezer section. They cost 79¢ for 4 ounces. I can buy a 10 pound bag of potatoes for 69¢. Much more spud for your buck.

By changing our lifestyle a bit, we can save a great deal. To get away from the need for convenience foods, there are a number of things that we can do. The first is to plan your meals, so that you aren't influenced by the fancy package and smells when in the store. Have a meal plan and specific shopping list. Buy only what is on your list. Say no to impulse items. Remember the marketing "tricks" that store designers play, and be smarter than the snares they devise. Stores bake items during peak shopping hours, arrange toys and attractive prepackaged meals at eye level, place high-priced snack foods at the check-out counter, etc.

The second thing we need to do is become comfortable with our kitchen. Plan on spending a little more time there, and learn to cook some things from scratch.

The last thing, but certainly not the least, is to buy items in bulk that you use often. This helps avoid the convenience items when you run out of your stock and rush to the store to get whatever will work in its place (but at a higher cost). If time is a problem for you, then cooking several meals ahead of time would be the most advantageous for you. I talk more about this later in the book, but wanted to mention some important tips about cooking in advance. By doubling recipes and freezing half for another day, I am able to build up a reserve of meals in the freezer. This is a homemade convenience food. You pull out a meal, and stick it in the microwave: just like the one that is four times more expensive in the pretty box.

Having meals in the freezer also keeps us from being tempted by those convenience meals. I often used to order a pizza ($20) when I was too tired to cook, or didn't have time to thaw the meat or cook from scratch. I have a frozen meal conveniently waiting on days like that.

Even meals made at home, but using a mix for seasoning or part of the preparation are costly. Let's take a look at a chicken and noodle dinner made from scratch and one made with some prepackaged ingredients.

Convenience item	Convenience cost	Homemade item	Homemade Cost
chicken (1 lb)	$1.58	chicken (1 lb)	$1.58
instant noodle mix	$1.29	noodles	50¢
frozen vegetables	$2.29	frozen vegetables	69¢
(sauce included)		homemade sauce	5¢
Total cost of meal	**$5.16**		**$2.82**

Keep in mind that this is only one meal. If most meals can have this type of cost variation, think of the difference you can make over a month (90 meals)!

The marketing of prepackaged mixes is deceptive as well. Many ads lead us to believe we are making a home-cooked meal when we use their package. This sly marketing is attempting to appeal to your instinct that homemade is better (and cheaper). Remember if the manufacturer did anything to "help" you make that recipe, you are paying them for that help.

GUIDELINE EIGHT: Cut Back On Meats

I HAD TWO REASONS for reducing the meat in my diet. My first was a monetary reason. Meats are a very expensive source of protein. They can range from $1–$7 per pound. Dried beans are an excellent source of protein, carbohydrates, iron, thiamin, and fiber. They cost very little, averaging about 25¢–49¢ per pound. They can be added to many types of dishes and are filling.

My second reason for reducing meat in our diet was health. I knew that we needed protein, but I knew that there were less expensive and more nutritious sources of protein. I also knew we ate more protein than we needed. Most adult Americans eat too much protein. The average serving for dinner is between 8 and 10 ounces of meat. Unless you are growing or pregnant, you probably need about half of that. But a plate looks a bit empty with a small cut of meat or chicken on it.

We are suppose to eat more vegetables and fruit than most of us are eating. Only 20% of Americans eat the recommended minimum of fruits and vegetables (five per day). By reducing our meat and stretching it with more vegetable and fruit, we can solve two problems at once. Dishes like stir-fry, fajitas, salads, stews, pot pies and casseroles call for many vegetables and grains with a smaller amount of meats. These cost less to prepare and are more nutritious for us. I also added more alternative proteins (dried beans, tofu, grains) to our diet. There are some very healthy meatless dishes that our family enjoys.
When I first cut out meats, I wanted to make sure we were getting the

protein and other nutrients we needed. I started my nutrient research with protein. I wanted enough, but not too much, since extra protein turns into fat. Who needs more fat?

I looked at the recommended daily needs for protein for each member of our family (available in most nutrition books) and added up the foods we usually ate to see if we were getting what we needed. We were, and had some to spare. My husband and I need 60 grams of protein per day, my 3 year old daughter, 40 gms. per day, and my eight-year-old son needs 52 gms. per day. These are averages for our family. People's need for protein increases (as much as three times) if they are ill, under stress, pregnant or nursing. Please consult a doctor before altering your diet. I looked at proteins that provide the most protein per pound, while still watching fat intake.

Proteins in Food Chart

Food Item	Quantity	Protein*	Fat
hamburger, 17% fat (lean)	3 oz. cooked	21 gm**	17 gm
chicken breast, skinless	3 oz. cooked	27 gm**	4 gm
chicken dark meat, skinless	3 oz. cooked	27 gm**	6 gm
turkey breast, skinless	3 oz. cooked	27 gm**	9 gm
cod fish (and most fish)	3 oz. cooked	28 gm**	5 gm
tuna	3 oz.	8 gm	7 gm
egg	1	6 gm	4 gm
yogurt, nonfat	1 cup	8 gm	0 gm
milk, nonfat	1 cup	8 gm	0 gm
peanut butter	1 tablespoon	4 gm	8 gm
peanuts	1/2 cup	18 gm	25 gm
hot dog	1	5 gm	13 gm
brown rice	1 cup cooked	5 gm	1 gm
tofu	4 oz.	10 gm	4 gm
dried beans, lentils	1 cup	15 gm	0 gm

*Please note that the protein and fat figures vary depending on the size of the item and how it is cooked. I also found that several nutrition books had different protein and fat values listed.

**There is some debate that we do not assimilate all of this protein in animal meat.

By looking at these figures, I realized we ate more protein than we needed. We could easily meet our needs with milk, some cheese and lots of grains. Meats could be a treat if we were really short on cash. Most countries use meat as flavoring or to enhance a dish. Their plates are 2/3 filled with complex carbohydrates, vegetables or fruit. Americans tend to feature the meat, and the rest is considered a "side dish."

I realized that we could cut back on the amount of meat we bought and ate, as well as include cheaper and healthier types of protein in the menu. I explored new ways to incorporate tofu into my recipes, and tried new dried bean recipes. I served smaller portions of meat at mealtime, filling the plate with grains, vegetables and fruits. I stretched the meat in dishes such as stir-fry, fajitas, etc. You can feed a family a steak dinner or lentil soup with whole grain rolls and they will get their protein needs. But they won't cost the same:

- *A steak dinner for 4 people costs $4–$5*
- *Hamburgers for 4 people costs $3*
- *Stir-fry for 4 people costs $2.50*
- *Rice and beans for 4 people costs $1.50*
- *Lentil soup for 4 people costs $1.25*
- *Spaghetti with meat sauce for 4 people costs $1.25*

My newfound zest for alternate sources of protein did not, however, cause me to become a complete vegetarian. There's more to dairy, egg and meat than just protein. Legumes and grains are a great source of most of the amino acids that we need to form proteins, but some nutritionists teach that some of the proteins and other elements that we need are lacking. This is why many legume dishes are combined with a small portion of high protein sources such as cheese (dairy), or a small portion of meat or eggs. Many people believe that the amino acids in grains combined with the amino acids in legumes forms a complete balance of the proteins that we need, and that dairy and eggs are not needed. Some dietitians argue with this finding, saying that the proteins available in grain/legume combinations are either incomplete or would require massive amounts in order to provide the necessary protein and other elements. This is especially true of growing children and pregnant women. These nutritionists also believe that certain trace elements needed in our diet can only be found in certain dairy, egg, or meat products. If a person never eats an occasional meat, egg, dairy or fish dish, they might be deficient in these elements. I am not an expert on diet and am merely sharing my findings. I suggest you discuss these issues with a licensed dietitian before changing your diet.

To start with meatless (or less meat) dishes, here are a few tips on bean and tofu preparations. There are some meatless recipes in the Some Great Recipes chapter.

DRIED BEAN PREPARATION SUGGESTIONS

1 cup of dried beans will expand into 2-1/2 cups after cooking.

There are several methods for soaking beans before cooking. Both methods are to wash the beans, and remove any beans that float when covered with water.

The overnight method:

Cover the beans with cold water (4 cups water to one cup beans), and let sit overnight. Drain, cover with water, and boil as directed.

The quick soak method:

Cover the beans in a pot with water. Boil for 10 minutes. Remove from the heat and place a lid on the pot. Let it stand for 1 hour. Drain and rinse the beans. Continue with your recipe.

Cooking times vary depending on the bean type:

- *white (or navy) beans and soybeans require the longest cooking time—up to 4 hours to cook.*
- *larger beans—2-3 hours to cook.*
- *smaller beans—1 hour to cook.*
- *lentils—1-1/2 hours to cook.*
- *lima beans cook—1/2 hour to cook.*

Storage

Since beans take a long preparation and cooking time, make several pounds of them and freeze in meal-size bags. Drop the frozen beans into the cooking dish or soup. They have a similar texture to canned beans.

TOFU PREPARATION SUGGESTIONS

Tofu is very inexpensive ($0.75–$1.39 per pound). It is even less expensive if you buy it directly from the tofu shops. These can be found in most Japantowns and Chinatowns.

Tofu provides the best source of usable protein. Fifty percent of it is protein, as compared to chicken at 21% and beef at 13%. This means you need less to obtain what you need. It also contains trace elements not found in any other plant. One example is choline, an essential element to the body. So far, it is only found in eggs, liver and soy beans. Anyone avoiding all animal proteins should learn to incorporate tofu or other soy bean products into their diet to be well balanced.

Tofu is very bland and can be incorporated into any dish. We have made custard with soft tofu, and used firm tofu in spaghetti sauces, in sandwiches, stir-fry, and casseroles in place of meat. It can be mixed with flour and spices to form a burger patty. Soft tofu can also replace any recipe that calls for cottage cheese, ricotta, or yogurt. It is low in fat. The firmer the texture of the tofu, the higher the protein content. It has the same amount of calcium as milk. Most supermarkets now carry it, making it easy to incorporate into your menus.

GUIDELINE NINE:
Waste Nothing

T HE "WASTE NOTHING" MENTALITY was prevalent in previous generations. Nothing was thrown out until it had been so used or recycled that it became useless for anything. Defining when something becomes useless varies from home to home.

Our grandparents were creative in finding uses for almost everything that came into their homes. Flour sacks were converted into dresses for the girls (the material was cotton and had a floral print on it) and dish towels. I have an antique quilt hanging in my home that is filled with small squares of those flour sacks. Jars that foods came in were reused to store their homemade items or to store small tools or bolts. Food that would be thrown out was fed to animals. Wood from broken crates was converted to furniture or toys. Old tires were cut and used to resole shoes. The list could go on because there was no end to their creativity and resourcefulness in recycling.

We can learn to stretch things a bit further. We were raised in a "disposable" age. Our parents wanted us to have it easier than they did. But with this blessing came a lost art. We don't know how to stretch things. We expect things to be ready made for us, and then we throw them out when we're done. Our generation is learning that there must be a better way. We recycle our cans and plastic to avoid filling up the landfills needlessly. We make things for ourselves. Don't be quick to throw out something without looking for another use. We reuse large food containers from the warehouse clubs for storing dry goods or small toys. We use sturdy boxes for storage. If the boxes are small enough, they can be used for diskette or cassette storage. Oatmeal containers make good small toy storage or a toy for the kids (see Crafts For Kids). The large laundry detergent boxes can be used to store baking mixes in (wash very well first). Milk cartons can be used for bird feeders or for freezing things in. There are books dedicated to this art of reusing. Check your local library.

We can apply this mentality to our food as well. Many leftovers can be made into another meal. The ends of bread loaves can be saved in the freezer for croutons, stuffing, bread pudding, or bread crumbs. Fruit about to turn bad can be made into smoothie drinks, pudding, popsicles, jam, jello or fruit breads. Bananas can be frozen in their skins until needed. Bits of vegetables and meats can go into a pot in the freezer to be used in soups, stews, pot pies, enchiladas, or stir-fry meals. Limp celery can be revitalized by soaking in ice water.

There is no end to the ways we can recycle wisely. I listed a few ideas to start you thinking of ways to reuse in your home. Explore the libraries for books on the never-ending ideas for item reuse. My favorite book on the subject of not wasting foods is the *Use-It-Up Cookbook* by Lois Willand. It lists every food you may encounter in alphabetical order. Each section lists uses for that food, recipes, and storage tips. It is very valuable for stretching food. More book titles on this subject are listed in the Resource section at the end of this book.

GUIDELINE TEN:
Institute a Soup
& Bread Night

H AVING SOUP AND BREAD for dinner once each week helps us stay within our food budget. Soups are inexpensive to make (when made from scratch), and they are nutritious. There are such a variety of soups in the world, you could try a new one every week and never repeat a soup recipe all year. Each country has some well-known soups in its cuisine. They probably have soups often for the same reason we do—it's inexpensive.

Most soups contain vegetables, some stock, and a starch of some type (potato, noodles, etc). These are the ingredients for a healthy meal. Check in your cookbooks for some recipes to get you started. There are cold soups, spicy soups, thick ones, thin ones. Just about anything your family likes can be found in soup form.

I avoid soup mixes or canned soups for the high costs as well as the fact that they are not as nutritious as a homemade soup. The canned or dried mixes have been cooked to death, highly salted, and laden with additives to keep it "fresh" for you. A soup and bread night made from scratch usually costs me $2 for all 4 of us. The same meal made from canned soup and store bought bread would run $4.25. To keep the cost down, I use leftover meat and vegetables that couldn't be used for anything else. I keep a bowl in the freezer for these leftovers. When the bowl is full, I can make soup or a stir-fry dish. Things that I might put in the bowl are a small leg of chicken that isn't enough for a lunch. The rest of the vegetables left in the pan after dinner. Some vegetables that are about to go bad if not used right away. Anything is usable for a stew, soup, or other dish. This is originally what soups and stews were—leftovers stretched into one more meal. If time is a real problem for you, try making your own soup mix and having it ready for dinner time. I have included some ideas on the following page on how to make a soup mix.

The bread that I serve with my soup is usually homemade biscuits. I serve cornbread once in a while as a treat. I try to bake bread if I have time. There are so many simple biscuit recipes in cookbooks. They take no time to mix or bake. For variety, add sour cream or yogurt instead of milk to make them fluffier. Add grated cheese to make them richer. Add herbs (dill or thyme) to make them tastier. Be creative with your mixing. For those with time constraints, make up a master baking mix (most cookbooks have one—my favorite is in the *More-With-Less Cookbook*). With these all you need to do at dinner time is add shortening and milk. If you really hate to mix up biscuits, the only cheap alternative that I have seen are the canned refrigerator rolls that go on sale for about 25¢ per can. They are full of preservatives, but are a quick solution.

My kids were not excited about the idea of soup night. Yours may not be either. Start them with something you think they'll like, such as a potato and cheese soup. When it's blended together, it's rich and cheesy. If they like wontons, try a wonton soup. If they like beans, try a black bean soup. If they like noodles, try chicken noodle soup. Start slow. Kids will adapt if they know that's all there is for dinner.

To help you get started, here are some of my favorite soup recipes.

INSTANT CREAM SOUP MIX

2 CUPS INSTANT MILK
3/4 CUP CORNSTARCH
1/4 CUP INSTANT CHICKEN BOUILLON
1 TSP. ONION POWDER
1/2 TSP. DRIED THYME
1/2 TSP. DRIED BASIL
1/4 TSP. PEPPER

Combine these and store in an airtight container.

To use for soup, combine 1/3 cup mix and 1-1/2 cups water. Bring to a boil while stirring often. Add a vegetable for more flavor, such as diced celery (for cream of celery soup), or some sliced mushrooms (for cream of mushroom soup), or some diced broccoli (for cream of broccoli soup).

To use for any recipe calling for a can of cream of mushroom, chicken or celery soup can be replaced with 1/3 cup mix and 1-1/4 cup water. Boil for a few minutes, stirring often.

QUICK POTATO CHEESE SOUP

1 CUP LEFTOVER MASHED POTATOES
1 CUP WATER
2 CUPS MILK
1/2 CUP CHEESE
1 ONION, DICED
1 TSP. SALT
1 TSP. PEPPER
2 T. FLOUR
1 T. BUTTER

In a saucepan, melt butter and fry onion until light brown. Stir in the flour and salt and pepper. Stir, forming a rue paste. Add water, stirring constantly. When mixed, add the rest of the ingredients. Stir while it thickens and the cheese melts.

Tip: you can replace the potato in most recipes with a turnip if desired. They require the same cook time and have similar texture.

VEGETABLE (OR FISH) CHOWDER SOUP

3 T. BUTTER
1/2 CUP CHOPPED CELERY
1/2 CUP CHOPPED ONION
1 CLOVE GARLIC, CRUSHED
1/2 CUP FLOUR
3 BOUILLON CUBES OR 1 T. GRANULES
3 CUP WATER
2 CUPS MILK
1-1/2 CUPS POTATOES, CUBED
1/3 CUP LEMON JUICE (OPTIONAL)
10 OZ. FROZEN CORN
PEPPER

Sauté celery, onion and garlic until golden. Add flour to form a paste. Add milk and water and bring to a simmer. Add potato, corn and bouillon. Simmer 12 minutes until potatos are tender. Add lemon juice if desired.

To make this a fish chowder, add 1 lb. of a cubed white fish (e.g. cod) with the water. Cook soup until fish flakes with a fork.

CREAMY TOMATO SOUP

1/4 STICK BUTTER
1 T. OLIVE OIL
1 ONION, DICED
2 GARLIC CLOVES , CRUSHED
1 T. BROWN SUGAR
2-1/2 LBS. RIPE TOMATOES, CHOPPED
4 CUPS CHICKEN STOCK
1 T. LEMON JUICE
1 CUP MILK

Melt butter and olive oil in large saucepan. Add onion and garlic and cook until golden. Blend in brown sugar and cook until melted. Add tomatoes, stock, and lemon juice. Reduce heat and simmer 45 minutes. Puree soup in processor if desired. Transfer back to saucepan, and add milk. Warm over low heat. Season with salt.

LEEK & POTATO SOUP

1-1/2 TSP. VEGETABLE OIL
3 LEEKS, THINLY SLICED
2 CLOVES GARLIC, MINCED
1/2 TSP. DRIED THYME LEAVES
6 CUPS CHICKEN STOCK
3 MEDIUM POTATOES, PEELED & CUT INTO SMALL CHUNKS
1/2 CUP MILK
SALT AND PEPPER TO TASTE

In a large saucepan, heat oil. Add leeks and cook until softened. Add garlic and thyme. Stir until golden. Pour in chicken stock and bring to a boil. Add potatoes. Simmer until potatoes are done. Remove from heat. Put soup in blender and blend. Stir in milk, salt and pepper.

BLACK BEAN SOUP

2 CANS (15 OZ.) BLACK BEANS
1 CAN (15 OZ.) STEWED TOMATOES
1 CAN CHICKEN BROTH
1 ONION, CHOPPED
1 GARLIC CLOVE, CRUSHED
SALT AND PEPPER
1 T. OREGANO
2 T. LIME JUICE

Combine in a large pan and simmer until cooked through. Add lime juice after cooked. Serve with homemade rolls or rice.

HOT AND SOUR CHINESE SOUP

1 CUP MUSHROOMS, SLICED
1 T. OIL
1 GARLIC CLOVE, CRUSHED
1 T. GINGER, MINCED
1-1/2 QUARTS CHICKEN BROTH
1 LB. FIRM TOFU, CUBED
3 T. CIDER OR RICE VINEGAR
2 T. SOY SAUCE
3 T. CORNSTARCH
1 TSP. PEPPER
4 GREEN ONIONS, SLICED

Heat oil in pan and sauté garlic, ginger, and mushrooms until garlic is light brown. Add broth and tofu and heat to a boil. In a small bowl mix the vinegar, soy sauce and cornstarch. Add to soup and continue to boil until soup is thick. Stir occasionally. Remove from heat and add green onions and pepper.

MY MOM'S BEST PEA SOUP

2-1/2 CUP CHICKEN BROTH
1 12 OZ. PACKAGE FROZEN PEAS, THAWED
1 TSP. TARRAGON
1 TSP. SALT
1 TSP. PEPPER
1 T. BUTTER
1 T. FLOUR
2 T. LEMON JUICE
1/4 CUP MILK

Put broth, peas, and spices in a blender and blend until smooth. It will be a bit chunky. In a pan, melt butter and add flour to form a paste. Pour the blender contents into the pan and bring to a boil. Boil, stirring occasionally, for 10 minutes. Remove from heat and add lemon juice and milk.

GUIDELINE ELEVEN: Cook Several Meals at Once and Freeze Them

T HERE HAVE BEEN MANY excellent books written on cooking and freezing meals in advance. It would be helpful to point out a few highlights of the concept of cooking in bulk. My two favorite books on the subject are *Once-A-Month Cooking* by Mimi Wilson & Mary Beth Laberborg, and *Dinner's In The Freezer* by Jill Bond.

Once-A-Month Cooking teaches you how the system works. These ladies do a good job of explaining the whole concept of cooking monthly, and give you several sample menus and recipes to follow. However, I did have some trouble converting their ideas into my recipes. When I read *Dinner's In The Freezer*, I breathed a sigh of relief. Jill Bond shows you how to take your recipes and convert them into a bulk cooking plan.

Both books share the same premise—the more you cook in bulk, the more you'll save. *Once-A-Month Cooking* suggests that you cook once a month. Jill Bond, however, goes one step further and suggests that you cook four to six months at a time. Both books explain how shopping and cooking in bulk will save you money and time in the kitchen. Cooking once a month takes between two and three days to do all of the shopping and food preparation for 30 days. Cooking once every four months takes only about twice that long. With both plans, you are shopping and preparing food up to the baking stage. For the evening meal, one merely thaws and bakes the meal. A few dishes are pre-cooked and only require reheating.

Preparing meals in advance saves you money in several ways. It will reduce your grocery bill, energy bill and save you time. The grocery bill will be less since you are able to buy foods in bulk. A 5 pound chub of hamburger or 10 pound bag of potatoes is cheaper than buying the same in lesser quantities. You also will spend less since you will be in the store less often. You won't pick up those impulse items each time you walk down the aisles.

Having meals in the freezer also saves by reducing the impulse to eat out or order a pizza. When you are running late, too tired to cook, or complaining that there is nothing to eat, you can do as Jill Bond does and say, "Dinner's in the freezer." This can be very handy for busy families or a working mom.

You also are saving energy costs by cooking in bulk. Cooking several dishes in the oven at once doesn't require more energy than just one dish would and reduces the oven's use threefold. Browning 10 pounds of hamburger instead of browning each pound alone saves five times the energy.

As for your time in the kitchen, it will be reduced considerably. Most of us spend an hour in the kitchen getting dinner ready. If all of the chopping and mixing is done, and all that is required is reheating or popping in the oven, consider how much more free time you will have.

I usually recommend that people try cooking in bulk slowly. It can be a bit overwhelming to plan a month of shopping and slicing. Just double or triple tonight's meal, and freeze the extra. Do the same tomorrow. And in a few days, you will have 2-3 weeks of meal stocked up. No extra sweat or planning. The reason I suggest the slow approach is to let you adjust to the idea of buying, cooking, and storing in bulk. If I sent you off to try the four-month plan, I think you'd close this book now. The four-month plan will save you the most money. But you need to first learn to plan and shop ahead. Once you do, you are ready to tackle larger amounts of planning and cooking.

STORAGE SPACE

People say they can't cook in bulk because they don't have an extra freezer. I got rid of my extra freezer four years ago when I learned it was consuming $15–$20 per month in electricity. I figured I needed that money elsewhere (times were really tight).

I only have the small freezer above my refrigerator. I have no difficulty freezing meals in this small space. I even store foods bought in bulk such as hamburger and chicken. To expand my freezer space, I cleared out all unnecessary items to make room for important things. I asked myself if it would be used soon, how much was it saving me, and could it be stored in the refrigerator instead. I then went to a hardware store and purchased a wire rack shelf for $3 that divided the freezer in half. This created more storage space.

My next step was to freeze in containers that used less space. A friend taught me that storing in large zippered freezer bags takes very little space. When filled with a meal and laid flat, it is only 1/2 inch thick. 10 can be stacked on top of each other, 2 stacks to a shelf. Plastic containers are too bulky to make my small space useful.

Some people have questioned the cost of my plastic bag usage, and wonder if I am using up my savings. I do not believe that I am. By using sales and coupons, I pay one or two cents per bag. Many can be washed and reused. If I used plastic boxes, I would need my extra freezer back to cook for more than two weeks at a time. I would have to use 1000 bags per month to pay for the electricity to run that extra appliance.

Other uses for freezer space:

- *I make several pizza dough crusts, wrap them individually and freeze them stacked on top of one another. Just thaw and let rise a little before baking.*
- *Do the same with pie crusts since they are no fun to make. Do it once and freeze.*
- *If I see a great sale on bread, I double wrap for longer freshness with a saved bread bag from a previous loaf.*
- *I save the ends of bread loaves and dried out bread and make bread crumbs or stuffing.*

• *Since beans take so long to soak and bake, I make a large batch and freeze them in meal size portions.*

FOOD SAFETY

One main concern when freezing in bulk is food handling and freezing. What foods were safe to freeze cooked or uncooked and how long was it safe to freeze them? I found some wonderful resources on these topics. There is a great book in the library called *Will It Freeze—An A To Z Guide To Foods That Freeze* by Joan Hood that lists each food alphabetically, giving freezing tips and storage times. I also located some useful resource people to answer questions on food preparation and storage.

FOOD SAFETY HOTLINES

U.S. Department of Agriculture
Meat and Poultry Hotline.. *(800)* **535-4555**
> *For meat and poultry handling and freezing guidelines. They can answer your question from 10–4pm EST, or you can hear automated answers 24 hours a day.*

FDA Seafood Hotline.. *(800)* **332-4010**
> *Prerecorded messages and publications 24 hours per day. You can talk to staff members from 12–4 pm EST.*

Food Safety and Nutrition Hotline............................ *(800)* **266-0200**
> *Offered by the Alliance for Food and Fiber. Prerecorded messages deal with food and safety issues.*

Safe Tables Our Priority (STOP)................................ *(800)* **350-STOP**
> *This group provides information on foodborne illnesses, and referrals to doctors, support groups, and lawyers. This was formed by parents of E.coli victims.*

**National Center for
Nutrition and Dietetics**.. *(800) 366-1655*

> *Registered dietitians answer questions and provide referrals on
> nutrients in food, food safety, vegetarian diets, cholesterol, etc.*

Milk Hot Line.. *(800) 949-6455*

> *Recorded messages, publications, and recipes. Also a mes-
> sage center to have a registered dietitian call you back.*

Land O' Lakes Holiday Bakeline............................... *(800) 782-9606*

> *From November 1 to December 24 they can answer your bak-
> ing questions. Callers receive a free holiday recipe booklet.*

Butterball Turkey Hotline... *(800) 323-4848*

> *From November through December they can answer your
> turkey baking questions*

Weber Grill Line... *(800) 474-5568*

> *During the summer months, staff are available from Monday
> through Friday, and prerecorded messages are available 24
> hours a day, to answer grilling questions.*

Food and Drug Administration (FDA)...................... *(301) 443-3170*

> *Information on foods, drugs, cosmetics, etc. sold in interstate
> commerce.*

Environmental Protection Agency (EPA)................. *(202) 382-4361*

> *Information on pesticides and safe levels on foods.*

Center For Disease Control... *(301) 443-5287*

> *Answers questions on illnesses.*

OTHER MANUFACTURER'S HOTLINES

Butter Buds	*(800) 231-1123*
Pillsbury	*(800) 767-4466*
Louis Rich Consumer Center	*(800) 722-1421*
Oscar Mayer	*(800) 222-2323*
Nature Made Vitamin Education Hotline	*(800) 276-2878*
International Olive Oil Council Hotline	*(800) 232-6548*
Braun	*(800) 726-0190*
KitchenAid	*(800) 422-1230*
Hitachi Home Electronics	*(800) 448-2244*
Welbilt Appliances	*(516) 365-5040*
Panasonic/Quasar/Technics	*(800) 545-2672*

Some Great Recipes

TO SUPPLEMENT my chapter on "Making Your Own Wherever Possible," I have gathered some helpful recipes. They are good in terms of flavor and nutrition, as well as providing savings. After each recipe, I have provided a cost analysis to compare what your homemade version is saving you. My cost is based on my price goals.

BREAKFAST IDEAS

Pancakes

This is a great savings over cereal. The cheapest and tastiest recipe that I have found is below. As I said before, don't be fooled into using baking mixes or other mixes. They are costly and save you no time over doing it from scratch. To save time and energy, cook twice the amount that you need and freeze them. They reheat well in the toaster or microwave. You can also freeze the batter in meal-size portions.

> 2 EGGS
> 2-1/2 CUP BUTTERMILK OR SOUR MILK
> 1 TSP. BAKING SODA
> 2-1/2 CUP FLOUR
> 2 TSP. SUGAR
> 4 TSP. MELTED BUTTER OR VEGETABLE OIL
> 3 TSP. BAKING POWDER
> 1 TSP. SALT
> 1/2 TSP. VANILLA

Beat together until smooth. Spoon on ungreased hot griddle. Flip over when bubbles appear.

COST ANALYSIS:(one dozen)

Homemade:	34¢
Mix:	90¢
Frozen Microwave:	$2.47

Maple Syrup

Homemade may not be as thick as store bought, because the manu-facturers use additives to thicken it. But this recipe is somewhat thick, and the flavor is great. To thicken yours, use less water or let it boil to a thicker consistency.

2 CUPS SUGAR
1 CUP WATER
1 TSP. MAPLE EXTRACT
1/2 TSP. VANILLA

Bring water and sugar to a boil, stirring constantly until it appears to be thickening. The longer you boil, the thicker it will become. It will also thicken some as it cools. Add flavoring as it is cooling. Store in the refrigerator.

COST ANALYSIS: (24 oz.)

Homemade:	11¢
Store Bought/(generic):	$1.59
Store Bought/(namebrand):	$3.19

Easy Donuts

If your kids like donut holes, but you don't want to pay $2.99 per dozen (like our bakery charges), try this quick and cheap recipe.

Buy a can of refrigerator rolls or biscuits when they go on sale for 25¢ per can. Cut a hole out of the center of each biscuit with something the size of a dime. I have used the lids of vinegar bottles or worcestershire sauce. If your family only wants donut holes, then cut each biscuit into quarters.

Pour vegetable oil so that there is 2 inches of oil in the pan. Heat oil to 350°. Deep fry until golden brown (only a few seconds on each side).

While still warm, glaze with one of the following glazes.

Glaze

> 2 CUPS POWDERED SUGAR
> 1 T. VANILLA EXTRACT
> 1/4 TSP. NUTMEG
> 3 T. MILK

Blend with a spoon until smooth. Dip the donut balls into the glaze and cool.

Chocolate Glaze

> 1 CUP SEMISWEET CHOCOLATE CHIPS
> GLAZE RECIPE ABOVE

Melt chocolate chips in microwave for 30–60 seconds, stirring often (don't cook too long or they harden). Add to the above glaze, and dip as directed.

COST ANALYSIS: (48 donut holes)

Strore Bought:	$12.00
Homemade:	40¢

Cinnamon Rolls

These taste like the famous cinnamon rolls sold in the malls.

Dough

> 1 T. DRY YEAST
> 1 CUP WARM MILK
> 1/3 CUP WHITE SUGAR
> 1/2 MELTED BUTTER
> 1 TSP. SALT
> 2 EGGS
> 4 CUPS FLOUR

Dissolve yeast in warm milk. Add the rest of the ingredients and mix well. Knead into a ball. Let rise until double in size. When ready, roll out to about 1/4 inch thick. Spread with filling as described below.

Filling

1/4 CUP BUTTER, SOFTENED
1 CUP BROWN SUGAR
3 T. CINNAMON

Spread butter on dough evenly. Sprinkle sugar and cinnamon over dough evenly. Roll dough up. Slice roll into 1 inch slices. Place on a greased pan. Bake 10 minutes at 400°

Icing

1/2 CUP BUTTER, SOFTENED
1-1/2 CUP POWDERED SUGAR
1 OZ. CREAM CHEESE
2 T. WHIPPING CREAM
1 TSP. VANILLA EXTRACT
PINCH OF SALT

Beat until fluffy. When rolls are hot, spread lots of icing on them.

Tip: Make these the night before needed. Skip the final rising step. Let rise overnight in the refrigerator. In the morning, bake.

COST ANALYSIS: (1 roll)

Store Bought:	$1.99
Homemade:	40¢

Nonfat Granola

This is my husband's favorite breakfast cereal—it even beats out the store bought version (in his opinion).

5 CUPS QUICK OATS
3/4 CUP BROWN SUGAR
1/3 CUP CONCENTRATED APPLE JUICE

1/2 CUP DRY MILK
1/3 CUP HONEY
2 T. CINNAMON
1/2 TSP. SALT
1/2 CUP DRIED FRUIT*

Mix sugar, juice, dry milk and honey in saucepan, and heat until sugar dissolves. Combine other dry ingredients in mixing bowl. Pour sugar mixture slowly over dry mixture and blend well. Place on cookie sheet and bake at 375° for 20–30 minutes, stirring every 10 minutes.

OPTIONS: Be creative by adding peanuts, sunflower seeds, coconut, sesame seeds, peanut butter or whatever else your family has handy to the mix.

COST ANALYSIS: (1 pound)

Store Bought:	$2.39
Homemade:	$1.00

*Note: You can lose your savings on this recipe by buying dried fruit. I found that the best way to add fruit and keep the cost down is to dry my own, or buy raisins in bulk. To dry your own, see the recipe below.

Dried Fruit

Peel and dice firm apples into the size of large raisins. Lay them in a single layer on a screen or on waxed-paper-lined cookie sheets. Put in oven and heat to 250°, then turn oven off. Do not open the oven door. Leave the pilot light on and leave the fruit in oven overnight.

COST ANALYSIS: (one pound)

Store Bought:	$3.99
Homemade:	79¢

Homemade Grape Nuts

3-1/2 CUPS WHOLE WHEAT FLOUR
1 CUP BROWN SUGAR
2 CUP BUTTERMILK OR SOUR MILK

1 TSP. BAKING SODA
PINCH OF SALT

Combine all of the ingredients in a mixing bowl and mix until smooth. Grease 2 large cookie sheets. Spread the mixture over the two sheets. Bake at 250° for 20–30 minutes, until golden brown. While still warm, crumble by grating on a large-holed cheese grater or in a food processor.

COST ANALYSIS: (48 ounces)

Store Bought:	*$6.50*
Homemade:	*$2.50*

Fruit Leather

Grind fruit in the blender and spread thinly on plastic wrap. Place in oven at 250° overnight or leave the light bulb on if you have a gas stove with pilot light. You can leave it outside for 1–2 days if covered by a screen to keep bugs out. Peel and enjoy!

COST ANALYSIS: (1 fruit roll up)

Store Bought:	*99¢*
Homemade:	*60¢*

Berry Jam

This is a tasty, quick and cheap way to avoid the high cost of jams. In the summer, when berries go on sale, make a large supply of this. Even in the winter when you run out of jam, buying frozen berries and making your own is cheaper than store bought. You can adjust the size of the recipe to whatever amount of berries that you have.

8 CUPS MASHED STRAWBERRIES
8 CUPS SUGAR

Cover berries with the sugar and let them sit until juice begins to appear. This is best if left overnight. Bring berries and sugar to a boil over medium heat. Boil 10 minutes. Check for thickness. If it starts to look thick as it runs off of the spoon, it's ready. Remove from heat and cool to room temperature. Put in jars and refrigerate. Experiment with other fruits or combinations of fruits (my favorite is 6 cups strawberries and 2 cups blackberries).

COST ANALYSIS: (3 10 oz. jars)

Store Bought:	$6.00
Homemade:	$2.25

No-Sugar Apple-Raspberry Jelly

These recipes use the natural sugars found in fruit juice.

1 (12 OZ.) CAN FROZEN APPLE JUICE CONCENTRATE
1 (12 OZ.) CAN FROZEN RASPBERRY JUICE CONCENTRATE
1 PACKAGE (2 OZ.) DRY PECTIN

Thaw juice and add water making 1 quart. Pour into large saucepan. Add pectin and dissolve over medium heat. Cook until boiling—stirring often. Increase heat to fast boil for 1 minute. Remove from heat and skim off the foam. Pour into sterile jars. Cover with lids and let cool.

Variations:

Add 1 package frozen raspberries (12–16 oz.) to fruit juice before boiling.

COST ANALYSIS: (24 ounces)

Store Bought:	$3.60
Homemade:	$2.50

Incredibly Fast Apricot Jam

This only takes a few minutes to prepare and the flavor is great. It is only cost effective if you can dry apricots yourself or buy them cheaply.

2 8 OZ. PACKAGES DRIED APRICOTS
2-1/2 CUPS ORANGE JUICE
3/4 CUP SUGAR
1/2 TSP. GROUND CINNAMON
1/4 TSP. GROUND GINGER
1 T. LEMON JUICE

In a large bowl, combine all ingredients. Cover tightly and microwave on high 10–12 minutes. Pour mixture in blender and puree until smooth. Pour jam into jars and let cool.

Variation:

For peach jam, use dried peaches and apple juice.

COST ANALYSIS: (40 ounces)

Store Bought:	$3.39
Homemade:	$2.20

SNACKS, BREADS, AND DRINKS

Instant 'Ade

Instead of buying the frozen concentrated drinks, such as lemonade or other "ades," try making a syrup base on your own and keeping it in the refrigerator.

The syrup base is made by putting the rinds (or skins) of selected fruit (lemon, lime, peach, ginger slices) into a cooking pot. Since pesticides are thickest on the skins, do this with organic fruits. Cover with one cup water and one cup sugar. Bring to a boil and boil for 10 minutes. Discard the rinds. Store in the refrigerator or freeze in ice cube trays for future drinks. Store the frozen cubes in a plastic bag.

To use, add a cup of water and a few drops of lemon juice (optional) to the syrup to taste.

COST ANALYSIS: (20 ounce drink)

Store Bought:	$1.89
Homemade:	20¢

Chocolate Syrup

1 CUP COCOA POWDER (UNSWEETENED)
2 CUPS SUGAR
1/4 TSP. SALT
1 CUP COLD WATER
1 T. VANILLA

Combine cocoa and sugar and blend until all lumps of cocoa are gone. Add water and salt and mix well. Cook over medium heat, bringing it to a boil. Keep boiling until thick, stirring to keep from overflowing.

Remove from heat and let cool. When cool, add vanilla. This is great for chocolate milk, hot cocoa, and ice cream topping.

COST ANALYSIS: (30 oz.)

Store Bought:	*$1.89*
Homemade:	*90¢*

My Chewy Granola Bars

1-1/2 CUP ANY GRANOLA
1/4 CUP HONEY
1/8 CUP CHOPPED PEANUTS, OTHER NUTS, OR CHOCOLATE CHIPS
1 EGG

Combine well and press into a greased 8x8 baking pan, about 1/2 inch thick. Bake at 350° for 20 minutes. Slice into bars after it cools.

COST ANALYSIS: (12 bars)

Store Bought:	*$3.59*
Homemade:	*60¢*

Soft Pretzels

3-1/2 CUPS FLOUR
2 T. SUGAR
1 TSP. SALT
2 PKGS. (1/4 OZ.) DRY YEAST
1 CUP WATER
1 T. SHORTENING
1 EGG YOLK

1 T. WATER
COARSE SALT

In a large bowl, heat 1 cup water to 110°. Add yeast first, then all other dry ingredients. Mix well and knead for 5 minutes. Set in a greased bowl and let rise until double in size. Punch down.

Divide the dough into 12 pieces, and roll each one into a long rope (18–20 inches). Shape into pretzels or other shapes. Place on a greased cookie sheet, and rest for 5 minutes. Mix egg yolk and 1 T. water. Brush on the pretzels, then sprinkle them with the salt. Bake at 375° for 15 minutes.

COST ANALYSIS: (12 soft pretzels)

Store Bought:	$3.29
Homemade:	70¢

Oatmeal Bread

(This is my favorite bread recipe)

2 PACKAGES (1/2 OUNCE EACH) ACTIVE DRY YEAST
2 CUPS QUICK-COOKING OATS
6 CUPS BREAD FLOUR
2 TSP. SALT
1/2 CUP BROWN SUGAR
1/2 CUP HONEY
2 T. VEGETABLE OIL
1-1/4 CUP WARM WATER
1-1/4 CUP WARM MILK

Dissolve yeast in water and add milk. Add sugar and honey and stir. Add the rest of the ingredients. Mix well. Knead for 5 minutes then let rise to double in size. Punch down then knead again. Let rise once more to double in size. Shape into loaves and let rise to double. Bake at 350° for 20 minutes.

COST ANALYSIS: (2 loaves)

Store Bought:	$4.98
Homemade:	$3.00

Peppermint Candy Canes

(From my great-grandmother Maggie's notebook)

> 2 CUPS SUGAR
> 1/2 CUP LIGHT CORN SYRUP
> 1/2 CUP WATER
> 1/4 TSP. CREAM OF TARTAR
> 3/4 TSP. PEPPERMINT EXTRACT
> RED FOOD COLORING

Cook sugar, water, and cream of tartar to a very hard ball stage. Remove from heat and add peppermint. Divide into two parts and add red coloring to one part and mix well. Pull pieces of each part to form ropes and twist red around the white to make candy canes.

COST ANALYSIS: (1 dozen)

Store Bought:	$1.29
Homemade:	50¢

Spiced Popcorn

> 1/2 CUP POPCORN KERNELS
> 2 TSP. CHILI POWDER
> 1 TSP. VEGETABLE OIL
> 1/2 TSP. GARLIC POWDER
> 1/4 TSP. SALT

Pour hot popped corn into large bowl. In a separate bowl, mix the rest of the ingredients. Toss chili mixture with popcorn until well coated.

COST ANALYSIS:

Store Bought:	$2.29
Homemade:	35¢

Cinnamon-Apple Lollipops

> 1 TSP. VEGETABLE OIL
> 10 LARGE CINNAMON STICKS, 2 INCHES LONG
> 1/2 CUP SUGAR

1/2 CUP LIGHT CORN SYRUP
1 TSP. CINNAMON
1/2 CUP WATER
2 T. APPLE JUICE CONCENTRATE

Brush a thin layer of oil over a baking sheet. Cut each cinnamon stick in half between the two curled edges. Lay cinnamon sticks on the baking sheet—they will be the stick of the lollipop.

In a pan, combine next four ingredients. Boil until a drop of syrup in ice water is hard and brittle. This takes about 10 minutes. Add apple juice. Continue cooking 3 minutes. Remove from heat and let stand. Spoon 1–2 tsp. of the syrup over the tip of each cinnamon stick and let stand until hardened.

You can replace the cinnamon sticks with lollipop sticks found at most baking supply stores.

COST ANALYSIS: (10 lollipops)

Store Brand:	$1.99
Homemade:	75¢

Popsicles

Popsicles bought at the store cost more than homemade, and usually have additives you may prefer to avoid. We started making them at home when we realized additives were affecting my son. We have explored some ways to make a tasty pop. Making them at home also is a great way to use yogurt and fruit that might spoil if left unused. Here are some ideas:

- *Take watermelon (or other fruits) that are getting a bit mushy, and puree them in a blender. This works well with watermelon, strawberries, and bananas. Fill some popsicle molds.*

- *Mix plain yogurt with fruit juice, or fruit extract and a bit of sugar. Pour in popsicle molds. This is only a good buy if the yogurt is on sale, or needs to be used soon.*

• *If you are going on a trip and have milk left in the frig that would spoil, mix it with a pudding mix (69¢) and pour in popsicle molds.*

COST ANALYSIS: (6 popsicles)

Store Bought:	
fruit juice popsicle	$1.40
Pudding Pops	$2.20
Homemade:	
fruit pureed in blender	40¢
frozen pudding mix	69¢
frozen yogurt	$1.47

Yogurt

If you really want to make a popsicle from scratch, you could start by making your own yogurt. It is about half the cost of store bought.

1 QUART MILK (WHOLE, LOWFAT, OR SKIM)
2 T. STORE BOUGHT PLAIN YOGURT (MAKE SURE THE SIDE OF CONTAINER SAYS "ACTIVE CULTURES" IN THE INGREDIENTS)

Start by heating a quart of milk until it is about to boil (don't let it!). Remove from the heat and put in a candy thermometer and wait until the temperature falls to 110°. Pour milk into a container with a lid (not metal). Take two tablespoon of the store bought yogurt and mix with the milk. Cover and keep warm (110°) for 10 hours. Keep it warm by either a) leaving in oven with pilot light and light bulb on, or b) setting on a heating pad and keeping a cloth over the top.

Store in the refrigerator when done.

COST ANALYSIS: (1 quart plain)

Store Bought:	$2.20
Homemade:	$1.15

Ice Cream Waffle Cones

1/4 CUP SUGAR
1/2 CUP FLOUR
1/8 TSP. SALT
2 T. CORNSTARCH
2 EGG WHITES
1/4 CUP VEGETABLE OIL
1/2 TSP. VANILLA
2 T. WATER

Combine the dry ingredients. Add liquid ingredients and blend until smooth. Lightly grease a griddle or pan and heat until water dances when dropped on it. Pour a small circle of batter in the center of the griddle and smooth into a large circle. Cook until brown and turn over for a short time until cooked on the other side as well.

Remove cake and quickly roll into a cone shape. Use a cone mold if you have one to roll it around. The ends should overlap and stick. Hold in place until cool, then remove from mold.

COST ANALYSIS: (6 cones)

Store Bought:	$2.89
Homemade:	60¢

Tortilla Roll Ups

This is my favorite hors d'oeuvre recipe.

1 PACKAGE 8" FLOUR TORTILLAS
2 PACKAGES CREAM CHEESE SPREAD, SALMON FLAVORED
1 SMALL CAN DICED BLACK OLIVES
1/2 RED ONION, DICED FINELY

Spread salmon flavored cream cheese over the surface of a tortilla. Sprinkle with olives and red onions. Roll up the tortilla as tightly as you can. Slice sections off (use a serrated knife for best results), about 1/2 inch thick. Lay them flat on a platter. They should look like pinwheels.

COST ANALYSIS: (3 dozen)

Store Bought:	$7.15
Homemade:	$4.35

Beef Jerky

1-1/2 LB FLANK STEAK

3/4 CUP WINE VINEGAR

1/2 CUP WORCESTERSHIRE SAUCE

1 TSP. SALT

1 TSP. PEPPER

1 CLOVE GARLIC (CRUSHED)

1/2 LARGE ONION (DICED)

Cut the steak into 1/2 inch thick slices. Combine the ingredients and let marinate in the refrigerator overnight. Lay the meat on a cookie sheet and bake at 150°. If you have a gas oven, that is about the temperature when the pilot light and oven light are left on.

Check in 2–3 hours. Turn over the pieces and dab the meat to absorb the grease. Cook another 2–3 hours or until all parts are dry. If moisture is still present, the meat still may be uncooked, and bacteria could grow—so use care to completely dehydrate the meat.

COST ANALYSIS: (3/4 pound)

Store Bought:	$11.89
Homemade:	$4.29

DESSERTS

Basic Cake

1 CUP SOFT SHORTENING
2 CUPS SUGAR
3 CUPS FLOUR
4 TSP. BAKING POWDER
1 TSP. SALT
1 CUP MILK
1/3 CUP WATER
1 T. VANILLA
3 EGGS (BEATEN TO FLUFFY)

Cream shortening and sugar in a small bowl. Sift flour, baking powder, and salt together in a separate bowl. In a third bowl, mix milk, vanilla, and eggs. Alternate adding the shortening, then the milk mixture to the flour, beating well after each addition.

Pour into a greased and floured 9x13 pan. Bake at 350° for 35–40 minutes, or until clean knife comes out dry when inserted in center of cake.

Decorating tips:

- *Avoid beating the cake batter too long, or it may crack.*
- *To avoid crumbs in the frosting as you spread, apply a thin layer of icing over the cake. Let it harden, then finish frosting.*
- *Freeze the cake before cutting into shapes.*
- *Decorate with colored coconut. Add a few drops of food coloring to a cup of shredded coconut in a bowl, and mix.*
- *For a butterfly shape: bake cake in a round pan. When cool, cut the cake in half, making two semi-circles. Place the curved sides together so they are just touching. It should look like a butterfly now.*
- *For a heart cake: bake cake in one square pan and one round pan. Place the square cake diagonally so it looks like a diamond. Cut the round cake in half and place one semi-circle on each side of the square.*

COST ANALYSIS:

Store Bought:	
Cake mix	$1.79
Bakery	$16.54
Homemade:	$1.15

White Bakery Frosting

2 BOXES POWDERED SUGAR (OR 9 CUPS)
1/2 CUP BUTTER (SOFTENED)
1/2 CUP SOLID VEGETABLE SHORTENING (CRISCO OR EQUIVALENT)
1/2 CUP HEAVY CREAM (OR MILK FOR A LESS RICH TASTE)
2 T. VANILLA
1/2 TSP. SALT

Blend sugar and shortenings together. Add cream slowly (just enough to get right consistency) and vanilla. Whip until fluffy. You can freeze the extra.

COST ANALYSIS:

Store Bought:	$2.29
Homemade:	$1.15

Chocolate Cake

1/4 CUP SOFT SHORTENING
1–1/2 CUPS BROWN SUGAR
2 EGGS
4 OUNCES SEMI-SWEET CHOCOLATE CHIPS
2 CUPS FLOUR
2 TSP. BAKING POWDER
1 TSP. SALT
1–1/2 CUPS MILK
1 T. VANILLA

Cream the shortening and sugar. Melt the chocolate in a pan placed on top of boiling water or use the microwave—but be careful not to over-heat. Add chocolate and eggs to the shortening mixture. Combine the milk and vanilla to this mixture.

In a separate bowl mix the flour, baking powder and salt. Slowly add the liquid mixture to the flour mixture, mixing well after each addition.

Pour the mixture into a greased and floured 9x13 pan. Bake at 300° for 30–45 minutes.

COST ANALYSIS:

Store Bought:	
Cake mix	$1.79
Bakery	$16.54
Homemade:	$1.65

Chocolate Frosting

   1 CUP CHOCOLATE CHIPS
   1 CUP BUTTER
   1/2 CUP HEAVY CREAM (IF SUBSTITUTING MILK, USE A BIT LESS)
   2-1/2 CUPS SIFTED POWDERED SUGAR

Melt the chocolate and butter in a large saucepan. Remove from heat and add cream. Mix well. Slowly add powdered sugar and blend. Whip with beaters for a more light texture.

COST ANALYSIS:

Store Bought:	$2.29
Homemade:	$1.55

Cookie and Cake Decorating Icing

   3 CUPS POWDERED SUGAR
   4 T. BUTTER
   1/2 CUP MILK
   1 TSP. VANILLA
   FOOD COLORING

Mix all except the food coloring until smooth. Divide the icing into smaller bowls. To each bowl, add a few drops of food coloring. Mix well. Spoon into baggies. Move the icing into a corner of the bag and twist to hold in place. Cut a tiny corner off of the bag to decorate with.

Cookie tips:

- *For crisper cookies, use butter for the shortening.*
- *For softer cookies, use vegetable shortening.*
- *To keep the edges from browning too soon, use a flat cookie sheet with no edges. To make one, turn your cookie sheet over.*
- *For browner cookies, use an aluminum sheet.*
- *For less brown cookies, use a glass Pyrex pan.*
- *To color sugar, put a few drops of food coloring in a bag with some sugar and shake.*
- *To make a hanging hole in a cookie, poke a hole before baking.*

COST ANALYSIS:

Store Bought:	$1.29
Homemade:	70¢

My Funnel Cakes

2 BEATEN EGGS
1-1/2 CUP MILK
2 CUP SIFTED FLOUR
1 TSP. BAKING POWDER
1/2 TSP. SALT
2 CUP COOKING OIL

Combine eggs and milk. Sift flour, baking powder and salt. Add to egg mixture and beat smooth. If it is too thick, add milk. If too thin, add flour. Heat oil to 360°. Pour 1/2 cup into funnel and drizzle into the oil, forming a circle with drizzles in the center. Fry until golden brown. Drain on paper towel and dust with powdered sugar.

COST ANALYSIS (each):

Store Bought:	$4.99
Homemade:	10¢

Lowfat Brownies

1/2 CUP FLOUR, SIFTED
1/2 CUP UNSWEETENED COCOA POWDER

1/4 TSP. SALT
2 LARGE EGGS
1 CUP GRANULATED SUGAR
9 T. UNSWEETENED APPLESAUCE
1 T. VANILLA

Grease and flour an 8-inch square baking pan. Combine dry ingredients in one bowl. In another bowl, whisk wet ingredients. Combine the two mixtures until just blended. Pour batter into pan. Bake for 25 minutes at 325°, or until done. Cool before cutting.

COST ANALYSIS: (1 dozen)

Store Bought Bakery:	$2.89
Homemade:	$1.29

Marshmallow Sauce

2/3 CUP SUGAR
1/4 CUP WATER
3 T. LIGHT CORN SYRUP
2 CUPS MARSHMALLOWS
1 TSP. VANILLA
DASH OF SALT

In a pan, cook water, sugar and corn syrup until simmering. Remove heat and mix in remaining ingredients. Stir until smooth.

COST ANALYSIS:

Store Bought:	$2.29
Homemade:	89¢

SPICES, MIXES AND SAUCES

The selection of store bought spice has grown the past few years. Many families buy seasoning mixes for meat. This has proven very profitable for the manufacturers of gourmet sauce mixes. They even put them right next to the meat, just to make it easier. Many of the mixes are simple combinations of spices you probably have in your cupboard. For example, spaghetti mixes seem to be popular. They cost between 60¢ and $1.99. You can save that by making your own with a little basil, oregano, thyme, garlic and onion. By looking in your recipe books, you can find what you need to add.

I also have found that some stores sell little bags of spices for 50¢ by an off-brand company. They are great for refilling empty spice jars. A new jar would cost between $2–$4.

There also are some bulk spices you can buy at the warehouse clubs. These are a bargain if you use the spice often.There are also some mail-order spice houses that sell by the 1/4, 1/2 and whole pound. Prices vary depending on the spice, but are usually less expensive if purchased in bulk.

Here are some of my favorite mixtures that we use regularly.

Spaghetti Herb Mix

1/2 CUP GARLIC POWDER
1/2 CUP ONION POWDER
1/2 CUP DRIED OREGANO
3 T. DRIED BASIL
3 T. DRIED THYME
3 T. SALT
2 T. SUGAR

Store in airtight container.

To use, blend 16 oz. of tomatoes with 4 T. of the mix.

COST ANALYSIS: (4 tablespoons/1 package)

Store Bought:	69¢
Homemade:	15¢

Curry Powder

Did you know you can make your own curry powder? Actually, there is no one recipe for curry powder. Everyone makes it their own way. Here's my way.

2 OZ. CORIANDER SEED
1/2 OZ. CINNAMON POWDER
1 OZ. PEPPER CORNS
1/4 TSP. NUTMEG
1 OZ. CUMIN SEED
1/2 OZ. CLOVES
1 OZ. LARGE CARDAMOM

Put in blender or coffee grinder and process as fine as possible. Store in an airtight container.

COST ANALYSIS:

Store Bought:	$2.29
Homemade:	50¢

Taco Spice Mix

1/4 CUP RED PEPPER FLAKES OR CHILI POWDER
1/4 CUP GROUND CUMIN
1/4 CUP OREGANO
2 T. CAYENNE
1/4 CUP GARLIC POWDER
1/4 CUP ONION POWDER
3 T. SALT
1 T. CLOVES

To use, add 2 tablespoons to one pound ground meat. Mix well and then cook. For dips, add 2 tablespoons to 1 cup sour cream or yogurt.

COST ANALYSIS: (2 tablespoons/1 package)

Store Bought:	79¢
Homemade:	25¢

Meat Marinade

2 T. VEGETABLE OIL
1 T. GARLIC POWDER
1 T. ONION POWDER
1 T. PEPPER

1 TSP. BROWN SUGAR
1 T. SOY SAUCE

Mix together and rub on meat. Let sit for at least 1/2 hour before cooking.

COST ANALYSIS:

Store Bought:	79¢
Homemade:	15¢

Buttermilk Salad Dressing

3 GARLIC CLOVES, MINCED
3/4 CUP MAYONNAISE
1/2 CUP BUTTERMILK (OR 1/2 CUP MILK + 1/2 TSP. VINEGAR)
1 TSP. DRIED PARSLEY FLAKES
1 TSP. ONION POWDER
1/2 TSP. SALT
1/2 TSP. PEPPER

Combine ingredients and mix until smooth. Chill for at least 30 minutes. This tastes best if left overnight before eating.

COST ANALYSIS: (24 oz.)

Store Bought:	$2.49
Homemade:	75¢

Caesar Dressing

1/2 CUP PARMESAN CHEESE
1/4 CUP + 2 T. OLIVE OIL
1/4 CUP + 2 T. VEGETABLE OIL
1/4 CUP FRESH LEMON JUICE
2 GARLIC CLOVES
1 TSP. WORCESTERSHIRE SAUCE

Mix all ingredients in a blender until smooth.

COST ANALYSIS (8 oz.)

Store Bought:	$1.59
Homemade:	50¢

Honey Mustard Dressing

1/2 CUP HONEY
1/4 CUP PREPARED MUSTARD
1–1/2 CUP SALAD OIL
2 CUPS MAYONNAISE
1/4 CUP CIDER VINEGAR
1/8 CUP CHOPPED ONIONS
CHOPPED PARSLEY
WORCESTERSHIRE SAUCE
PINCH OF SALT

Blend all ingredients until smooth.

COST ANALYSIS: (1 quart)

Store Bought:	$2.49
Homemade:	$1.65

The Best Bleu Cheese Dressing

1 CUP SOUR CREAM
1 TSP. DRY MUSTARD
1 T. BLACK PEPPER
1 T. VINEGAR
1/2 CUP MILK
1/2 TSP. SALT
1/2 TSP. GARLIC POWDER
1 TSP. WORCESTERSHIRE SAUCE
1 1/3 CUPS MAYONNAISE
4 OZ. BLEU CHEESE

Blend all ingredients (except blue cheese) well. Add blue cheese in very small pieces and stir well. Let sit 24 hours before using for maximum flavor.

Lowfat alternative: replace sour cream with plain yogurt.

COST ANALYSIS: 26 oz.

Store Bought:	$5.60
Homemade:	$2.14

Garlic Croutons

2 T. BUTTER
1/4 CUP OLIVE OIL
2 LARGE GARLIC CLOVES, PRESSED
4 BREAD SLICES, CUT INTO 3/4 INCH CUBES

Melt 2 T. butter, olive oil and garlic in saucepan. Place bread cubes in a large mixing bowl. Add butter mixture and mix well. Place on baking sheet and bake at 350° until bread is brown and crisp (20 minutes).

COST ANALYSIS: 24 oz.

Store Bought:	$2.49
Homemade:	$1.15

Barbecue Sauce

1 CUP KETCHUP
1 TSP. SALT
1 TSP. PEPPER
3 CLOVES GARLIC, CRUSHED
1/4 CUP BROWN SUGAR
1 TSP. DRY MUSTARD (OPTIONAL)
1/4 CUP VINEGAR (CIDER OR WINE)

Combine all ingredients in saucepan. Let simmer for 15 minutes.

COST ANALYSIS: 12 oz.

Store Bought:	$2.29
Homemade:	$1.15

Steak Sauce

2 CUPS KETCHUP
2 GARLIC CLOVES, MINCED
2/3 CUP CHOPPED ONION
1/2 CUP EACH LEMON JUICE, WATER, WORCESTERSHIRE SAUCE AND VINEGAR
1/4 CUP SOY SAUCE
1/4 CUP PACKED DARK BROWN SUGAR
2 T. PREPARED MUSTARD

Combine the ingredients in a saucepan and boil. Reduce to a simmer and cook for 30 minutes. Refrigerate the leftovers.

COST ANALYSIS 24 oz.

Store Bought:	$7.50
Homemade:	$1.75

MAIN DISHES

Many people have asked what my family eats for dinner. Most have assumed that we live on casseroles and noodles. We enjoy a variety of foods and flavors. I was determined not to give up my mealtime variety in order to live on less money. I have found ways to make our favorites, but do it for less. I have selected a few of our favorites to share.

Pizza

Few of us make our own pizza anymore. Making one from scratch is easy and can cost significantly less than buying one. Here is my favorite recipe:

Dough

1 CUP WARM WATER
1 PKG. DRY YEAST
1 TSP. SUGAR
3 CUPS WHITE FLOUR
2 T. OIL (PREFERABLY OLIVE)
1 TSP. SALT

In a bowl, mix the yeast, sugar and water, stirring to dissolve the yeast. Let it rest 5 minutes. Add the other ingredients. Knead the dough on a floured board, adding more flour until it's not sticky. Don't add too much flour, or the dough will become hard. Place in a bowl and cover, letting it rise from five minutes to two hours, depending on the texture you would like your dough. The longer you let it rise, the more bread-like the dough will become. Punch down the dough and shape into a large pizza. For a good crust, cook on a metal cookie sheet.

Dough variations: mix herbs into the dough. Add 1 T. oregano or dill, and 1 tsp. garlic powder.

Topping

Top with any of these combinations, then bake at 450° for 15 minutes.

- *spaghetti sauce, mozzarella cheese, pepperoni, sausage, olives, or onions.*

- *for a vegetarian pizza, top with tomatoes, marinated artichoke hearts, olives, onion and bell peppers.*

- *for "California" style pizza, brush the dough with olive oil, then sprinkle with basil and oregano.*

- Sprinkle some chicken pieces and just a bit of mozzarella cheese over the herbs. A few slices of fresh tomato add some color and flavor.

- *for Italian zest, spread pesto over the crust, then layer a thinly sliced zucchini and a few tomatoes. Sprinkle with basil, salt and pepper.*

- use Monterey jack cheese if mozzarella is not available or price prohibitive.

COST OF DISH (serves 4):   *65¢ (crusts only)*

Leftover Bread Meal

3 CUPS DRIED BREAD (BROKEN INTO CUBES)
4 EGGS
1 CAN (32 OZ.) SPINACH
1/2 CUP SHREDDED CHEESE
1 TSP. SAGE
1 TSP. THYME
1 TSP. GARLIC POWDER
1/2 ONION, DICED
1 TSP. SALT

Let the bread dry out by leaving it out overnight. Break it up into a large mixing bowl. Add the rest of the ingredients. Mix well. Put into a greased loaf pan. Bake at 350° for 1 hour.
Slice to serve.

COST OF DISH (serves 4):   *$1.89*

Poor Man Steak

1 LB. GROUND BEEF OR TURKEY
1/2 CUP CRUSHED SALTINE CRACKERS
1/2 CUP WATER

2 TSP. SALT
1 TSP. PEPPER

Combine all of the ingredients in a bowl and mix well. Pat into thin patties and fry in ungreased frying pan.
Serve as they are, or add a sauce for variety.

COST OF DISH (serves 4): $1.15

Messy Chicken

1 POUND CHICKEN (ABOUT 4 LEGS WITH THIGHS)
SALT
2 T. OIL
1 ONION, FINELY CHOPPED
2 CLOVES GARLIC, PRESSED
1 TSP. GROUND CINNAMON
1/2 TSP. GROUND CLOVES
2 T. BROWN SUGAR
3 SMALL YAMS OR SWEET POTATOES (1 LB. TOTAL), PEELED, CUBED
1 TART GREEN APPLE, PEELED, CORED AND DICED
1 CAN (EIGHT OUNCES) TOMATO SAUCE
1/2 CUP CHICKEN BROTH
2 T. APPLE CIDER VINEGAR

Salt the chicken lightly. Heat oil in a frying pan and brown chicken. To the drippings in the pan add onion. Cook until golden. Add garlic, cinnamon, cloves, and brown sugar. Add back to pan the chicken, yams, apple, tomato sauce and chicken broth. Simmer for 45 minutes. Remove chicken, yam and fruits to a serving dish. Stir in vinegar. Stir over heat until sauce is thickened. Pour over chicken.
Serve over rice.

COST OF DISH (serves 6): $4.45

Leftover Chicken Italian Meal

1 8 OZ BAG OF NOODLES
1 LB. LEFTOVER COOKED CHICKEN, CUBED
1 CAN STEWED TOMATOES
1 T. VEGETABLE OIL (OLIVE PREFERABLY)
1 GARLIC CLOVE, CRUSHED

1 TSP. OREGANO
1 TSP. THYME

Boil noodles until done. Drain. In a skillet, heat oil, garlic and herbs. Toss in tomatoes and chicken. Heat thoroughly. Toss with noodles. Serve with salad. For variation, add frozen corn or diced potatoes to sauce.

COST OF DISH (serves 4): **$2.70**

Pot Pie

1 CUP CHICKEN BROTH
1 ONION, DICED
1 POTATO, PEELED AND CUBED
2 CARROTS, PEELED AND CUBED
3 RIBS OF CELERY, CUBED
1 CUP LEFTOVER COOKED CHICKEN, CUBED
2 T. RUE (1 T. BUTTER + 1 T. FLOUR, MELTED TOGETHER)
1 TSP. SAGE
1 TSP. OREGANO
1/2 TSP. PAPRIKA
1/2 TSP. PEPPER

Combine all of the ingredients in a pan and stir over heat. Put in a baking dish and spoon the crust on top. Bake 375° for 45 minutes.

Quick Spooned-On Crust

1 CUP FLOUR
1-1/2 TSP. BAKING POWDER
1/2 TSP. SALT
1 CUP MILK
1 TSP. VINEGAR
1/2 CUP MELTED BUTTER
1/2 TSP. PEPPER

Combine ingredients and spoon over chicken.

COST OF DISH (serves 4): **$2.70**

Fast Food French Fries

My kids enjoy the taste of McDonald's fries, but I can't drop in a few times a week like we used to. So, I learned how to make my fries taste like theirs.

2 CUPS WARM WATER
1/3 CUP SUGAR
2 LARGE POTATOES, CUT IN STRIPS

Dissolve sugar in warm water. Place sliced potatoes in the water and let set for 15–30 minutes. Heat oil (enough to cover potatoes) to 350°. Dry off all visible water from potatoes and place in oil. Cook for one minute then remove. This cooks the insides. Let oil return to 350°. Place potatoes back into the oil and cook until golden brown. Remove, drain and salt to taste.

COST OF DISH (serves 2–4):   *40¢*

Onion Rings

1 EGG
1/4 CUP MILK
1 CUP ALL-PURPOSE FLOUR
1/2 TSP. BAKING POWDER
VEGETABLE OIL OR SHORTENING, FOR FRYING
1 EXTRA-LARGE ONION, SLICED INTO RINGS 1/2-INCH THICK
SALT, TO TASTE

Mix eggs and milk in a bowl. In a separate bowl, mix together flour and baking powder. Heat shortening in a large pot until very hot.
Dip the onion into the egg mixture and then into the dry mixture. Re-dip into the egg mixture and then back into the dry mixture. Put rings into the hot oil in small groups to keep the temperature hot.
Cook the onion rings until golden brown. Remove and drain on paper towels. Salt to taste and eat right away.

COST OF DISH (serves 4–6):   *55¢*

THE INTERNATIONAL CORNER

Below are some of my favorite international dishes. I enjoy a variety of dishes in my cooking, so I'll share my easiest and cheapest to make.

Fajitas

> 1/2 LB. CHICKEN BREAST (OR BEEF STRIPS), SLICED
> 1/2 ONION, SLICED
> 3 CLOVES GARLIC, DICED OR MASHED
> 2 T. OIL
> 2 LIMES (OR LEMONS), SQUEEZE FOR JUICE
> 1 TSP. CHILI POWDER
> 1/4 TSP. GROUND CUMIN
> 1/2 TSP. SALT
> 1/2 TSP. PEPPER
> 6 LARGE FLOUR TORTILLAS

Toss meat and ingredients together and marinate for at least 1/2 hour (the longer the better).

To cook, layer the chicken and larger pieces of vegetables on a broiler pan, and place in broiler for a few minutes, or until chicken is done. Discard juices. The meat also can be grilled over the barbecue, or pan fried. If pan frying, add all of the vegetables and juices to the pan with the meat.

Serve on flour tortillas, and roll up like a burrito. For a fancier meal, garnish with guacamole, salsa, sour cream, lettuce or grated cheese.

Time Saver: Prepare the meat and marinade in bulk (but do not cook) and freeze in meal size pouches.

COST OF DISH (serves 4): **$3.70**

Indian Curry

> 2 CUPS MEAT (CAN BE LEFTOVER PIECES OF CHICKEN, BEEF OR FISH)
> 1 CUP CHICKEN BOUILLON
> 5 T. BUTTER
> 1/2 CUP MINCED ONION
> 6 T. FLOUR
> 4-1/2 TSP. CURRY POWDER
> 1-1/4 TSP. SALT
> 1-1/2 TSP. SUGAR

1/4 TSP. GINGER
2 CUPS MILK
1 TSP. LEMON JUICE
1 CUP DICED APPLE

Melt butter. Add onion and cook until golden. Add the next five ingredients and stir into a paste. Add bouillon and milk. Cook, stirring until thickened. Add meat and lemon juice before serving. Serve over brown rice.

Condiments that are tasty (if available):

CHUTNEY   RAISINS
PEANUTS   COCONUT
PINEAPPLE   HARD BOILED EGGS
PICKLES (SWEET)

COST OF DISH (serves 4): $2.75

Chinese Pineapple Chicken

1 LB. CHICKEN BREAST
1 TSP. CORNSTARCH
PEPPER
1 GARLIC CLOVE
OIL
3 TSP. SOY SAUCE
1 SMALL CAN PINEAPPLE CHUNKS
2 T. WATER
1 T. CORNSTARCH

Mix chicken with 1 tsp. cornstarch, pepper, garlic clove, and 1 tsp. soy sauce. Fry chicken in a little oil until under done. Add pineapple (save the juice for later). Simmer 3 minutes. Set aside. Mix 2 tsp. soy sauce, water, leftover pineapple juice and 1 T. cornstarch. Add sauce to chicken in pan and cook until thick. Serve on rice.

COST OF DISH (serves 4): $3.50

Mushroom Chicken

> 4 PIECES BONELESS CHICKEN THIGHS
> 1 CAN CREAM OF MUSHROOM SOUP
> 2 T. LEMON JUICE OR VINEGAR
> SEASON WITH SALT, PEPPER, OREGANO AND THYME IF AVAILABLE.

Arrange chicken in frying pan. Pour ingredients on thighs and cook (covered) on medium heat for 30–40 minutes (or until done).
Put chicken on serving platter, and make gravy with the sauce left in the baking dish (add 2 T. flour to sauce, and stir on low heat; add milk to thin).

Serve with mashed potatoes.

> *COST OF DISH (serves 4):*   *$1.69*

Chicken Salad

> 3 PIECES OF BONELESS CHICKEN THIGHS, BOILED, CUBED, COOLED
> 1 BUNCH GREEN ONIONS, DICED
> 1 HEAD ROMAINE LETTUCE
> 1 CUP ROASTED PEANUTS

Dressing:

> 1/2 C. MAYONNAISE (OR LOWFAT YOGURT)
> 1/4 C. HONEY
> 2 T. PLAIN MUSTARD

Combine salad ingredients in a salad bowl. Prepare dressing and toss with salad.

> *COST OF DISH (serves 4–6):*   *$4.99*

Sandy's Cheese Chile Rellano Puff

> 1 7-OZ. CAN WHOLE GREEN CHILIES
> 8 OZ. MONTEREY JACK CHEESE
> 6 EGGS
> 3/4 CUP MILK
> 1 T. FLOUR
> 1 TSP. BAKING POWDER
> 1/2 TSP. GARLIC SALT

Grease a small baking pan. Lay down the chilies and cover with 4 oz. jack cheese. Combine the rest of the ingredients. Pour over chilies. Top with rest of cheese. Bake at 350° for 30 minutes.

COST OF DISH (serves 4): $2.00

MEATLESS DISHES

Thai Noodle Meal

1/2 LB. PASTA
1 CUP DICED VEGETABLES (USE LEFTOVERS-CARROTS, CELERY, PEPPERS, BROCCOLI)
1/2 CUP CHUNKY PEANUT BUTTER
3 T. SOY SAUCE
1 T. VINEGAR (WINE, CIDER, OR RICE)
1/2 TSP. HOT PEPPER FLAKES (OR TABASCO SAUCE OR ANY HOT SEASONING MIX)
1/2 CUP WATER

Microwave the vegetables until just tender. Cook noodles and drain. Set aside. Mix the rest of the ingredients in a saucepan. Heat and stir until well mixed and warm through. Toss with pasta. Serve with a salad.

COST OF DISH (serves 4): $1.50

Anne 's Squash Casserole

6–8 ZUCCHINI, SLICED THINLY
2 EGGS
1 PACKAGE SALTINES, CRUSHED
SALT, PEPPER, TO TASTE.
1/4 CUP GRATED CHEESE

Cook squash and drain. Mash with a fork. Stir in the eggs. Add enough saltines to absorb liquid. Bake 325° for 45 minutes. Top with grated cheese.

NOTE: For a non-dairy diet, replace the eggs and cheese with 3/4 cup mashed tofu.

COST OF DISH (serves 4): $ 2.29

Vegetarian Chili

> 1 T. OIL
> 2 CLOVES GARLIC, MINCED
> 2 ONIONS, CHOPPED
> 2 (16 OZ.) CANS STEWED TOMATOES
> 2 (16 OZ.) CANS KIDNEY BEANS
> 2 GREEN PEPPERS, CHOPPED
> 1 (6 OZ.) CAN TOMATO PASTE
> 3–6 T. CHILI POWDER
> 1 T. CUMIN SEEDS OR 1 TSP. GROUND
> 1 TSP. DRIED OREGANO
> 1 TSP. SALT
> 1/2 TSP. PEPPER

Combine oil, garlic and onions in large pan. Heat until tender. Stir in the rest of the ingredients and simmer for 30 minutes.

Serve with corn bread.

> **COST OF DISH (serves 6–8): $ 3.60**

My Favorite Vegetable Pancake

> 3 CUPS VEGETABLES, GRATED OR FINELY CHOPPED
>   (USE WHAT YOU HAVE OR WHAT'S IN SEASON. FOR A NICE FLAVOR, USE MUSH-
> ROOMS, ZUCCHINI, AND LEEKS)
> 1 CUP POTATO, GRATED
> 1/2 ONION, GRATED OR DICED
> 4 EGGS
> 1/2 TO 1 CUP BREAD CRUMBS (IF UNAVAILABLE, USE SALTINES OR FLOUR)
> SALT AND PEPPER TO TASTE
> 1/2 CUP GRATED CHEESE (CHEDDAR ADDS BEST FLAVOR, BUT ANY WILL DO)

After grating the vegetables, let sit for 15–30 minutes. Drain the grated vegetables of all visible water. Add eggs and seasoning, then add bread crumbs until a dough forms. Add cheese and mix well. Form patties and fry in ungreased non-stick pan. You can use a regular pan, but may require a bit of oil to reduce sticking.

NOTE: For a non-dairy diet, you can replace the egg and cheese with 1 cup mashed tofu and 1/2 cup flour.

> **COST OF DISH (serves 4–6): $ 1.95**

Chinese Noodles

1/2 LB. THIN NOODLES
1 LB. EXTRA FIRM TOFU
1/2 CUP CUBED CARROTS
1/2 CUP FROZEN PEAS
2 T. VEGETABLE OIL
1/2 ONION, DICED
3 GARLIC CLOVES, CRUSHED
1/8 TSP. RED PEPPER FLAKES OR TABASCO SAUCE TO TASTE (OPTIONAL)

Sauce

1/2 CUP KETCHUP
1/2 CUP WATER
2 T. SOY SAUCE
2 T. VINEGAR (WINE, CIDER, OR RICE)

Cook noodles and drain. Set aside. Heat the oil in a pan (or wok) and fry onion, garlic and red pepper until onion is golden while constantly stirring. Add all remaining ingredients and sauce. Heat until warm. Toss with noodles

COST OF DISH (serves 4): $2.25

Easy Microwave Lasagna

8 LASAGNA NOODLES, UNCOOKED
1 28–32 OZ. JAR SPAGHETTI SAUCE
2 T. WINE VINEGAR
1 16 OZ. CAN SPINACH + LIQUID
16 OZ. RICOTTA OR COTTAGE CHEESE
1 EGG
1 TSP. PEPPER
1 TSP. OREGANO
1 TSP. GRANULATED OR DEHYDRATED GARLIC
1 CUP GRATED MOZZARELLA CHEESE

In one bowl, combine spaghetti sauce, vinegar, spinach and the liquid from the can. In another bowl, combine ricotta, egg and spices. In two 8 x 8 pans, spread 1/2 cup sauce on the bottom of each pan. Then take 2 uncooked noodles and break to fit across bottom of each pan. Spread 1/2 cup of egg mixture over noodles. Sprinkle a little cheese across the egg mixture. Cover with 1/2 cup spaghetti sauce. Repeat layers in the same order, ending with sauce on top. Cover with plastic wrap.

Cook one pan 30 minutes on medium power in the microwave. When done, let sit covered (for added flavor) while the other cooks.

NOTE: For a non-dairy diet, replace the ricotta cheese and egg with 2–1/3 cup (18 oz.) mashed tofu, and omit mozzarella cheese or use tofu cheese.

COST OF DISH (serves 4): $4.10

Tofu Nuggets

My kids like these as an alternative to chicken nuggets.

> 1 LB. TOFU, FIRM
> BREAD CRUMBS

Cut the tofu into one inch cubes. Roll in bread crumbs and lay on a microwave safe plate. Heat for 30 seconds to one minute. Season with favorite herbs (my kids like oregano and garlic salt).

COST OF DISH (serves 6–8): $1.15

Huevos Rancheros

> 1 T. VEGETABLE OIL
> 1 MEDIUM ONION, DICED
> 1 GLOVE GARLIC
> 1 CAN (15 OZ.) STEWED TOMATOES
> 2 T. CHILI POWDER
> 1 T. OREGANO
> 6 EGGS
> 1/2 CUP GRATED CHEESE

Heat oil in a skillet and sauté onions and garlic until tender. Add tomatoes and spices. Stir to combine. Add eggs onto the sauce, leaving a bit of space between them. Do not break the yoke. Cover pan and simmer, so eggs will poach. When eggs are done, scatter cheese over the eggs and wait until melts. Serve on rice.

NOTE: For a non-dairy diet, replace the eggs with firm tofu (cubed), and omit cheese or replace with tofu cheese.

COST OF DISH (serves 4): $2.25

Beans and Rice

Rice:

Prepare rice for four people. Add 1/2 cup salsa before serving and stir.

Beans:

> 1 32-OZ. CAN OF PINTO BEANS
> 2 OZ. MONTEREY JACK CHEESE (GRATED)
> 1 T. VINEGAR (CIDER)
> 1 T. OIL
> 3 GREEN ONIONS, DICED
> 1 T. CAYENNE PEPPER

Put oil in a frying pan. Pour in beans. Mash beans with a fork in the saucepan. Add cheese. Heat and stir constantly. When smooth, add vinegar and cayenne, stir and remove from heat. Garnish top with green onion slices

Variations: For a non-dairy diet, replace the cheese with tofu cheese. For a truly authentic meal, prepare salad using salsa as the dressing.

COST OF DISH (serves 4): $ 1.50

Spaghetti with Zucchini sauce

> 1 28-32 OZ. JAR SPAGHETTI SAUCE
> 1 LB. ZUCCHINI, SLICED AND CUT IN HALF
> 1/2 CUP GRATED CHEESE
> 1/2 LB. SPAGHETTI NOODLES

Cook noodles and set aside. Combine zucchini and sauce in a saucepan and heat until zucchini are cooked. Toss with noodles and cheese.

NOTE: For a non-dairy diet, replace the cheese with tofu cubes.

COST OF DISH (serves 4): $ 2.80

White Beans and Tomatoes

1 LB. WHITE BEANS (SOAKED OVERNIGHT)
4 CUPS VEGETABLE BROTH OR WATER
2 BAY LEAVES
1 ONION, CHOPPED
4 CARROTS, SLICED
4 STALKS CELERY, SLICED
2 TSP. BROWN SUGAR
4 GARLIC CLOVES
7 CUPS TOMATOES, CHOPPED
1/4 CUP LEMON JUICE

Combine stock, beans and bay leaves in a large pot. Simmer for 1 hour. Drain half of the stock. Add the rest of the ingredients and return to a boil. Cook for 45 minutes, or until thick. Remove from heat and stir in lemon juice. For added flavor, let sit overnight, then reheat before serving.

COST OF DISH (serves 4): $ 4.50

Terry's Lentil Rice Casserole

3 CUPS WATER OR VEGETABLE BROTH
3/4 CUP LENTILS, UNCOOKED
1/2 CUP BROWN RICE, UNCOOKED
2 ONIONS, CHOPPED
1 T. DRY BASIL
1 T. OREGANO
1 TSP. THYME
1 TSP. GARLIC POWDER (OR 2 CRUSHED GARLIC CLOVE)
1 T. VEGETABLE SEASONING SPICE
1 T. SALT
1/2 CUP GRATED CHEESE, TOFU CHEESE, OR YOGURT (OPTIONAL)

Combine in a casserole dish. Bake at 300 for 2–1/2 hours. Remove from heat and top with cheese or yogurt before serving.

COST OF DISH (serves 4): $1.55

Bean and Tofu Stew

1 T. OIL
1 ONION, CHOPPED
1 BELL PEPPER, CHOPPED
1 GARLIC CLOVE, CRUSHED
1 28 OZ. CAN CHOPPED TOMATOES
1 15 OZ. CAN PINTO BEANS, DRAINED
1 15 OZ. CAN WHITE BEANS, DRAINED
1/4 CUP WORCESTERSHIRE SAUCE
1 T. VINEGAR
1 TSP. CHILI POWDER
1/2 TSP. SALT
1/2 TSP. THYME
1/2 TSP. SAGE
1/2 TSP. PEPPER
1/2 TSP. GARLIC POWDER
2/3 CUP RICE, UNCOOKED
6 OZ. FIRM TOFU, CUBED

Sauté first four ingredients until tender. Add remaining ingredients (except tofu) and simmer. Continue to cook, stirring occasionally until rice is tender. Add tofu and heat for 5 minutes.

COST OF DISH (serves 4): $3.15

Sandwich Spread

1 15 OZ. CAN BEANS (GARBANZO, BLACK OR PINTO), DRAINED AND RINSED
2 T. YOGURT OR TOFU
1/2 TSP. CHILI POWDER
2 T. ONION, CHOPPED
1 T. LEMON JUICE (IF USING BLACK BEANS, LIME JUICE IS BETTER)
1 GARLIC CLOVE, CRUSHED

Place all ingredients in a blender and blend until smooth. This can be mashed by hand in a bowl. Spread on pita pockets or whole wheat bread, or dip with tortilla chips.

COST OF SPREAD: 89¢

Tofu Mayonnaise

   8 OZ. TOFU
   3 T. LEMON JUICE
   8 TSP. OIL
   1/2 TSP. SALT

Combine all ingredients in a blender and mix until very smooth. Store in the refrigerator.

   COST OF DRESSING: *50¢*

GIFTS FROM THE KITCHEN

Grandma's Spiced Nuts

   1 CUP SUGAR
   1/2 CUP HALF AND HALF OR CANNED MILK
   1 TSP. CINNAMON
   1 TSP. NUTMEG
   1 TSP. VANILLA
   3 CUPS WALNUT PIECES

Mix sugar and milk in saucepan and boil until a hard ball is formed when a drop is placed in cool water. Remove from heat and add nutmeg and vanilla. Add walnuts and mix well. Spread nuts on waxed paper, separating each nut. Let dry.

   COST OF GIFT: *$ 2.85*

Sponge Candy

   THIS IS FUN TO MAKE WITH KIDS, SINCE IT BUBBLES AND FROTHS.

   1 CUP SUGAR
   1 CUP DARK CORN SYRUP
   1 T. DISTILLED WHITE VINEGAR
   1 T. BAKING SODA

Line a cake pan with foil on the bottom and sides, extending it over the edges, and grease foil. Mix sugar, syrup, and vinegar in saucepan over medium heat. Cook until candy thermometer reaches 300°. Stir occasionally. Turn off heat and add baking soda right away. Stir until mixed evenly. Quickly pour into greased pan. Let it cool completely. Lift out using foil as handles. Break the chunk into smaller pieces. Can store for one week.

COST OF GIFT: 95¢

Orange-Chocolate Truffles

1/3 CUP HEAVY CREAM
1/4 CUP BUTTER
6 OZ. SEMI-SWEET CHOCOLATE CHIPS
1 TSP. ORANGE EXTRACT
UNSWEETENED COCOA POWDER

Mix cream, butter, and chips in a double boiler until melted. Don't let it boil or burn. Remove from heat. Stir in orange extract. Pour into a baking pan and chill for 30 minutes or until firm. Scoop small amounts to make small balls. You should be able to make 2 dozen balls. Roll balls in your hands then roll in cocoa powder.
Store in refrigerator for up to two weeks.

COST OF GIFT: $1.25

Be Wary of Warehouse Clubs

WAREHOUSE CLUBS are large, plain, unattractive buildings filled with things we think we need. I know people who do 90% of their shopping at warehouse clubs, believing they're being thrifty. Unfortunately, warehouse clubs have to be used as carefully as grocery stores. They don't have the lowest price on everything, regardless of what other people have said.

These stores are actually private clubs. You pay an annual membership fee for the privilege of shopping there. Almost anyone can join through their credit union, professional club, employer, or by having a business license. Membership fees are currently $38 in California. These clubs have sprung up across the nation with PriceCostco and Sam's Club owning most of the stores.

Some frugal experts have claimed that these stores only make profit by charging membership fees. I don't believe that this is true. The membership fees help them, but are not the only source of income. From what I have read, seen for myself by shopping around, and by talking to various employees of these stores, I believe these stores make their profits four ways. Their profits come from membership fees, low overhead (no-frills buildings and minimal staff), by high volume sales of special deals, and high mark-up on certain items.

Many of the items they sell are the cheapest around. Sometimes they only make a few dollars on an item. This is especially true of the appliances, office equipment and home entertainment equipment. Even though they make a small amount on each item, they sell hundreds of thousands of that one item (at all stores combined) which adds up to a healthy profit. And have you noticed that they only sell one brand and type of that item? This isn't because it's the best one on the market (believe me–I have returned many of these "bargains"). They obtain a good deal on a particular model, and want to move it as quickly as possible. If they sold any other brands or models of that item, they would have extra inventory to carry. That is lost profit. Hence, there is only one brand of non-chlorine bleach, one brand of bandage, one brand of vacuum, one phone/fax machine, etc.

After comparing prices of many like items at our local warehouse clubs with local grocery store prices, I have shortened the list of what I buy at warehouse clubs to only 10–15 items. This list changes as they change their prices. I have found that about 30% of the warehouse club's goods are cheaper than anywhere else, another 30% are the same as you can get on sale elsewhere, and the last 30% are actually more expensive.

Many of the warehouse club bulk packages are the same price as individual packaged items on sale at grocery stores. This is true of some cereal, diapers, bread, tuna, potato chips, milk, plastic bags, some frozen foods, fresh meats, and paper products (when comparing paper products, don't forget to take the thickness into consideration—1 or 2 ply, as well as the number of sheets per roll). Watch the local stores' bulk section. Many are carrying a section of bulk packaged items, like a warehouse club. Many times the local store will charge the same or less than the warehouse club.

Knowing your prices is crucial at these stores. The packages are larger than we are used to and it's harder to determine if it's a good deal. Some things are cheaper, but many things actually are more expensive than at regular grocery stores. Taking your price list helps. Many people fall into the trap of thinking everything is less than at a regular grocery store, so they buy whatever they need or want. This can be financially deadly. For example, one warehouse club sells their own brand of paper products at 2.5 times higher (that's 250%) than a name brand equivalent at local stores. I also think that the quality of these paper products are inferior to items I buy elsewhere for less. The warehouses have to recover their profits somewhere. These higher prices are scattered throughout the store so that you can't avoid a certain area. A good example of this is name brand over-the-counter drugs. Most name brand drugs are cheaper at the warehouse clubs than the same name brand at a grocery store. But you have to watch out. On my last visit I compared the price of Bayer aspirin, and found that the unit price of the jumbo size I would have to buy at the warehouse club cost more than at the local grocery store. You need a calculator and your price list for safe maneuvering.

When we compare items, we must not forget the store brand equivalents sell at a much lower price. Warehouse clubs mainly sell well advertised name brands. This alone makes their prices higher on many items. Name brand items tend to be more expensive than an off brand. A warehouse club will usually be cheaper if you only compare that name brand to its price at a grocery store. But we must not forget the great alternatives found in generic and store brands. Occasionally a warehouse club will sell their own brand. Many of these brands are equally as good as the name brand equivalent. Some off brands are even the same item. Many companies buy items from these name brand corporations and sell them under their own label. These items may be surplus or close to their expiration date. Stores make more profit when they sell their own brand. They have eliminated the middle man, and can sell for less than any competitor and still make a good profit. The warehouse clubs know this and are beginning to add more of their own brands. The quality of most store brand items is improving greatly. They know you won't settle for less, so they continually improve the flavors, textures and durability of their goods.

Warehouse clubs should be a tool like other resources. They should be used only for those things they are good for. When I stick to this plan, I stay within my budget. But I am as easily tempted as anyone. And warehouse clubs can be very tempting. I tend to "over buy foods" when I shop at these stores. I buy more of some item than we normally need, and the food is consumed as quickly as when I buy less—even when we aren't hungry. If it's there, we eat it. I am tempted by the convenience foods that are cheaper than at a grocery store. But I must remind myself that making them is even cheaper—and healthier.

I often am asked if joining a warehouse club is worth the cost. I believe the answer is, "Yes." It is a fair question that each person needs to calculate. I don't like that I have to pay to shop at a store, but if I am careful about what I buy I come out ahead every year. If you watch your prices, and only buy those items that are good buys, it is worth it. Otherwise, if you buy everything that your home needs at this type of store, you could be paying $38 a year to spend as much as you would at a regular grocery store.

To help you maneuver through the aisles of these warehouses, I have listed good buys and bad buys at warehouse clubs. I tried to pick commonly used items. This is by no means a complete list. This will help start your own research. Remember that each store's prices may vary, and prices change weekly in some areas. The details of these comparisons are listed at the end of this chapter in a table format. The prices in the column titled "Grocery Store Sale Price" are the prices that I usually pay for that item.

GOOD DEALS AT A WAREHOUSE CLUB

- *most over-the-counter drugs*
- *spices*
- *light bulbs*
- *batteries*
- *most peanut butters*
- *most lunch meat*
- *Hershey's Cocoa Powder*
- *cheese*
- *some salad dressing*
- *oats*
- *most crackers*
- *most frozen meat*

There are other good buys at warehouse clubs I didn't list because they are convenience items I don't buy. This list includes sodas, candy, gum, canned spaghetti, and baking mixes.

BAD DEALS AT A WAREHOUSE CLUB

- *vegetable oil (store brand is cheaper and no different)*
- *certain over-the-counter drugs*
- *plastic bags*
- *paper products (toilet paper, paper towels, tissues)*
- *juice boxes*
- *boxed cereal*
- *potato chips*
- *milk*
- *certain salad dressing*
- *spaghetti*
- *flour*
- *sugar*
- *eggs*
- *margarine*
- *chocolate chips*
- *fresh meat*

WAREHOUSE CLUB PRICES

MEDICINE

Name Brand	Unit Count /Weight	Total Cost	Warehouse Unit Cost	Grocery Store Sale Price
Bayer aspirin	180 ct./325 mg.	$13.99	$0.08/pill	$0.06/pill
Safeway brand aspirin	100 ct./325 mg.	$0.99		$0.01/pill
Tylenol Extra Strength	250 ct./500 mg.	$11.49	$0.05/pill	$0.06/pill
store brand acetaminophen	1000 ct./500 mg.	$6.59	$0.006/pill	$0.04/pill
Excedrin	275 ct.	$11.59	$0.04/pill	$0.08/pill
Advil	250 ct.	$11.99	$0.05/pill	$0.07/pill
store brand ibuprofen	1000 ct.	$9.99	$0.01/pill	$0.05/pill
Children's Tylenol	96 ct./80 mg.	$5.99	$0.06/pill	$0.12/pill
generic children's acetaminophen				$0.08/pill

Name Brand	Unit Count /Weight	Total Cost	Warehouse Unit Cost	Grocery Store Sale Price
Sudafed	130 ct./30 mg.	$10.99	$0.08/pill	$0.14/pill
generic pseudoephedrine	24 ct./30 mg.	$3.39		$0.14/pill
Nyquil Liquid	2 x 10 oz.	$7.99	$0.40/oz.	$0.46/oz.
Robitussin	12 oz.	$6.49	$0.54/oz.	$0.68/oz.
store brand cough syrup	6 oz.	$3.49		$0.58/oz.
Dimetapp	12 oz.	$8.49	$0.71/oz.	$0.89/oz.
Centrum vitamins	200 ct.	$11.29	$0.06/pill	$0.06/pill
store brand vitamins	500 ct.	$11.99	$0.02/pill	$0.05/pill
Crest Tartar Control	3 x 8.2 oz.	$6.39	$0.26/oz.	$0.33/oz.
Tums	400 ct.	$7.99	$0.02/pill	$0.02/pill

LAUNDRY DETERGENT

Name Brand	Unit Count /Weight	Total Cost	Warehouse Unit Cost	Grocery Store Sale Price
Fresh Start	10 lbs. 8oz.	$11.99	$0.10/load	$0.10/load
All	200 oz.	$6.79	$0.14/load	$0.14/load
Trader Joe's detergent	64 oz.	$3.49		$0.11/load

HOUSEHOLD ITEMS

Name Brand	Unit Count /Weight	Total Cost	Warehouse Unit Cost	Grocery Store Sale Price
Ziploc bags	138 ct./quart	$7.99	$0.06/bag	$0.02/bag
Ziploc bags	189 ct./gallon	$7.99	$0.04/bag	$0.02/bag
Store brand paper towel	8 x 96 ct./2 ply	$6.99	$0.005/ply	$0.004/ply
Viva Versatile paper towel	12 x 75 ct./1 ply	$9.99	$0.01/ply	$0.02/ply
store brand tissues	8 x 96 ct./2 ply	$6.29	$0.005/ply	$0.005/ply
Kleenex tissues	8 x 78 ct./3 ply	$8.29	$0.005/ply	$0.002/ply
store brand toilet paper	24 x 450 ct./2 ply	$8.89	$0.0005/ply	$0.0005/ply
Northern Quilted	30 x 420 ct./2 ply	$11.79	$0.004/ply	$0.003/ply
light bulbs (100 watt)	10 x 2 ct.	$5.30	$0.27/bulb	$0.50/bulb
batteries, size AA, alkaline	40 batteries	$8.99	$0.22/battery	$0.37/battery
Cascade gel	120 oz.	$4.89	$0.04/oz.	$0.04/oz.

GROCERIES

Name Brand	Unit Count /Weight	Total Cost	Warehouse Unit Cost	Grocery Store Sale Price
juice boxes	24 boxes/8 oz.	$8.89	$0.37/box	$0.33/box
Capri Juice packs	4 x 10 ct./box	$7.59	$0.19/pack	$0.19/pack
Skippy peanut butter	5 lb. jar	$5.59	$0.07/oz.	$0.08/oz.
Adam's Peanut butter	4 lb. jar	$5.99	$0.09/oz.	$0.12/oz.
Cheerios cereal	35 oz.	$5.89	$0.17/oz.	$0.13/oz.
Spoon Size Shredded Wheat	48 oz.	$7.39	$0.15/oz.	$0.14/oz.
Frosted Flakes	47 oz.	$6.89	$0.15/oz.	$0.14/oz.
Post Raisin Bran	47 oz.	$5.59	$0.12/oz.	$0.12/oz.
Trader Joe's Wheat Squares	15.3 oz.	$1.69		$0.11/oz.
oats	9 lb.	$5.25	$0.58/lb.	$0.75/lb.
Oscar Meyer bologna	1 lb.	$1.20	$1.20/lb.	$0.99/lb.
Butterball turkey slices	2 lb.	$5.99	$2.99/lb.	$4.50/lb.
Louis Rich turkey lunch meat	4 x 12 oz.	$6.65	$1.66/pkg.	$2.29/pkg.
Foster Farms turkey franks	4 x 1 lb.	$3.69	$0.92/lb.	$0.79/lb.
Star-Kist tuna	6 x 6 1/4 oz.	$3.49	$0.58/can	$0.50/can
Pringles	4 cans	$4.19	$1.05/can	$0.99/can
Nabisco Graham Crackers	32 oz.	$3.25	$0.10/oz.	$0.12/oz.
milk (2%)	2 x 1 gallon	$4.27	$2.13/gl.	$1.99/gl.
store brand gourmet coffee	2 lb.	$6.99	$3.49/lb.	$3.49/lb.
Knotts Berry Farm blackberry jam	42 oz.	$3.75	$0.09/oz.	$0.15/oz.
Knotts Berry Farm grape jelly	64 oz.	$2.59	$0.04/oz.	$0.04/oz.
Smucker's strawberry jam	3 lb.	$3.39	$0.07/oz.	$0.07/oz.
Kraft macaroni & cheese	12 pack	$6.95	$0.58/box	$0.49/box
store brand macaroni & cheese				$0.33/box
Best Food mayonnaise	64 oz.	$4.65	$0.07/oz.	$0.08/oz.
store brand mayonnaise				$0.06/oz.
Bernstein's Italian Dressing	33 Oz.	$3.49	$0.11/oz.	$0.22/oz.
Hidden Valley Ranch Dressing	36 oz.	$4.79	$0.13/oz.	$0.11/oz.
spaghetti	5 lb.	$4.59	$0.92/lb.	$0.50/lb.
Mazola vegetable oil	1 gallon	$5.99	$0.05/oz.	$0.07/oz.
Wesson vegetable oil	1.25 gallon	$6.69	$0.04/oz.	$0.06/oz.
store brand vegetable oil	64 Oz.	$2.99		$0.04/oz.
Olive oil	2 liter	$9.19	$4.59/liter	$5.89/liter
Crisco	6 lb.	$4.99	$0.83/lb.	$0.83/lb.
Pillsbury flour	25 lb.	$6.49	$0.26/lb.	$0.16/lb.
sugar	10 lb.	$3.19	$0.32/lb.	$0.19/lb.
Hershey's Syrup	72 oz.	$4.29	$0.06/oz.	$0.06/oz.
homemade chocolate syrup				$0.03/oz.

Name Brand	Unit Count /Weight	Total Cost	Warehouse Unit Cost	Grocery Store Sale Price
Hershey's Cocoa Powder	23 oz.	$4.99	$0.22/oz.	$0.30/oz.
Log Cabin Maple Syrup	36 oz.	$3.39	$0.09/oz.	$0.09/oz.
homemade maple syrup				$0.01/oz.
onion powder	20 oz.	$2.89	$0.14/oz.	$0.20/oz.
cinnamon powder	16 oz.	$2.99	$0.19/oz.	$1.05/oz.
vanilla extract	16 oz.	$5.99	$0.37/oz.	$0.99/oz.
eggs large grade A	18 eggs	$1.48	$0.08/egg	$0.05/egg
cheddar cheese	2.5 lb.	$4.75	$1.90/lb.	$1.99/lb.
Precious mozzarella cheese	5 lb.	$9.25	$1.85/lb.	$1.99/lb.
Imperial margarine	5 lb.	$2.99	$0.60/lb.	$0.39/lb.
butter	3 lb.	$2.99	$0.99/lb.	$0.99/lb.
Nestle's Chocolate Chips	4 lb.	$5.99	$0.12/oz.	$0.12/oz.
store brand chocolate chips	12 oz.	$0.99		$0.08/oz.

FRESH MEATS

Name Brand	Unit Count /Weight	Total Cost	Warehouse Unit Cost	Grocery Store Sale Price

Beef & Pork

fresh extra lean hamburger	1 lb.	$1.69	$1.69/lb.	$0.99/lb.
fresh tri-tip roast	1 lb.	$2.79	$2.79/lb.	$1.58/lb.
fresh pork chops	1 lb.	$3.79	$3.79/lb.	$2.99/lb.

Chicken Breasts

fresh–boneless, skinless	6 lb.	$17.84	$2.99/lb.	$2.99/lb.
frozen–boneless, skinless	4 lb.	$11.99	$2.99/lb.	$2.99/lb.
frozen–boneless, skin on	4 lb.	$9.99	$2.50/lb.	$2.58/lb.

Stretch The Season

G ARDENING is the number one hobby in America—
but it is also a good way to cut grocery costs. I
know friends who have converted one of the yards
(back or front) of their home into a large vegetable garden.
These friends grow their own produce and don't buy any
produce all summer. One friend calculated the cost of each
organic tomato that she grew at 1¢ each. That's a great
savings from the store bought cost of 15–20¢.

If you don't have a large yard, make a small garden. Many magazines
have special editions on how to use a small space to produce vegetables. A four by eight foot raised garden box can produce an abundant
harvest. I use every space, including the fence where I grow berry
vines. Don't limit yourself to the dirt on the ground. I also have used
hanging pots to grow produce. I had a series of pots running around
the eave of my house in which I grew strawberries, carrots, cherry
tomatoes and herbs. If you have no yard at all, many cities offer a
community plot. There are sometimes two to three lots per city. They
give you a large plot of your own, all the water you need, and free
mulch for an annual fee (our city charges $60 per year). This comes
to $5 per month. For fresh, organic produce, you can't spend less than
that at a store.

For those who want to try a hand at converting their yard into a garden, here are some cost-saving tips. Fertilizer is free from horse sta-
bles and chicken farms. Mulch is free in some cities if they have a
recycling program. In my area mulch is free at a local public farm,
Emma Prusch farm. Make your own compost in a small container.
There are books at the library on how to do this. For bedding borders,

collect rocks at a local creek. Seeds go on sale in March at most stores. You can order them through the mail by catalog. Some people save seeds from their own garden harvest. Be careful on storage—they don't like it too hot or too cold. Hybrid seeds yield poor crops in their second year. Seeds can be bought cheaply and in the quantity you need. One store in our area called Common Ground (2225 El Camino Real, Palo Alto, CA 94306) sells seeds in bulk. You put as many spoonfuls as you want into bags provided. Or you can order seeds by mail. Common Ground buys some of their seeds from Bountiful Garden Seeds (707-459-6410).

To decide which vegetable or fruit to grow, look at the amount of yard needed and the yield the item will give you. For example, a zucchini bush takes up a very large area, but a tomato vine does not. There are even hybrid plants that grow several vegetables and fruits together. Some smart farmers have grafted fruit tree limbs of several types to one trunk, allowing a good harvest off of limited space. I have even heard of tomato plants with potato plants grafted so that above ground you get one type of vegetable and below ground you get another.

The main challenge of growing your own produce, or having friends who do, is the sudden surplus of one item. What do you do with 30 pounds of tomatoes all at once? One way to avoid this problem is to plant in shifts. Plant one row one week, another the next week, etc. so that they ripen in shifts as well. If you are the recipient of bushels of produce from generous friends, there are ways to stretch the produce to last all year. Remember that our farming ancestors learned this art. That's how they had food all year round. Preserving is done by salting, pickling, canning, freezing, and drying. I recommend these methods if you have abundance of any food item. You won't need to buy that food item most of the year.

To preserve my bounty, I bake a bunch of meals or snacks from that one food item and then freeze them. For example, I'll made a ton of jam, zucchini bread, and tomato sauce. I then have what I need all year. Below are some tips I selected from my notes. They are mainly for excess zucchini, pumpkins, tomatoes and fruits. I picked these produce items because they are the most commonly grown in home gardens.

ZUCCHINI

Zucchini Relish

7 ZUCCHINI, CHOPPED UNPEELED
4 LARGE ONIONS, CHOPPED
1 LARGE SWEET RED PEPPER, CHOPPED
1 CAN (4 OUNCES) CHOPPED GREEN CHILIES
3 T. SALT
3-1/2 CUPS SUGAR
3 CUPS VINEGAR
1 T. GROUND TURMERIC
4 TSP. CELERY SEED
1 TSP. PEPPER
1/2 TSP. GROUND NUTMEG

Combine first 5 ingredients and let rest overnight. The next day, rinse the relish and drain. Bring the remaining ingredients to a boil. Add relish to the pot and simmer. While it's hot, put into jars. Leave a small space at the top. Fit lids on tight. Follow proper canning procedures for sealing if relish is to be stored.

Zucchini Bread

3 EGGS, BEATEN
1-1/2 CUP SUGAR
1/4 CUP OIL
1/2 CUP CONCENTRATED APPLE JUICE
3 TSP. VANILLA
3 CUP GRATED ZUCCHINI
3 CUP FLOUR
1 TSP. BAKING SODA
4 TSP. BAKING POWDER
1 TSP. SALT
3 TSP. CINNAMON
1/2 TSP. NUTMEG
1/2 TSP. ALLSPICE

Combine all of the above ingredients and mix well. Pour in greased and floured pan and bake at 350° for 50–60 minutes.

Remove from the oven and cool before slicing.

Other good uses for zucchini are zucchini and potato pancakes and spaghetti sauce with zucchini.

TOMATOES

Tomato Tips

- *Select firm tomatoes with dark color. They should feel heavy as light tomatoes can be mealy and bland.*
- *Keep at room temperature.*
- *Very ripe tomatoes should be refrigerated.*
- *If you have unripened tomatoes on the vine and frost is imminent, pull up the whole vine and hang it upside down in a cool dark place. They will ripen slowly over a few weeks.*
- *When cooking fresh tomatoes, avoid aluminum pans. The acid in the tomatoes may react and form an unpleasant taste.*
- *In cooked tomato dishes, a pinch of sugar helps the flavor.*
- *Wash tomatoes right before use. Washing before storage can cause spoilage.*
- *To peel a tomato, try these two easy ways. First, place the tomato in boiling water for 30 seconds, then put into cold water. The skin will come right off. The other requires putting the tomato on the end of a fork, and holding it over a gas flame. Turning until the skin blisters. Pull the skin off.*
- *Freeze any tomatoes not needed. Freeze them whole and when fully ripened.*
- *Dry tomatoes by using the recipe below.*

How to sun dry a tomato

6 LBS. RIPE TOMATOES (PREFERABLY ROMA—LESS WATERY)
2 T. SALT
3 CUPS OLIVE OIL

Preheat oven to 200 degrees. Slice tomatoes lengthwise and arrange on racks or screens. Sprinkle with salt. Bake until 3/4th their original size with no signs of moisture. This will take 8–9 hours. Remove from oven and cool one hour. Pack in pint-size jars and cover completely with oil. Seal tightly. Store up to eight weeks.

Salsa

> *1 T. OLIVE OIL*
> *2 ONIONS, DICED*
> *2 CLOVES GARLIC, MINCED*
> *1 GREEN PEPPER, DICED*
> *1 RED PEPPER, DICED*
> *2–3 CUPS DICED FRESH TOMATOES*
> *3 TSP. WINE VINEGAR*
> *1/4 TSP. BLACK PEPPER*
> *1 T. FRESH CILANTRO, CHOPPED*
> *1/4 TSP. CAYENNE PEPPER*

(All of these portions can be varied to suit your taste.)

Heat oil and sauté onion, garlic, green pepper, and red pepper. Add tomatoes, and rest of ingredients to pan and stir. Remove from heat immediately. Serve with tortilla chips or on top of refried beans or corn bread.

Fried Green Tomatoes

Dip slices of green tomato in flour. Fry in oil. For best flavor, fry in bacon drippings.

PUMPKIN

These recipes call for canned pumpkin, because it goes on sale in the fall. More savings can be obtained by buying surplus pumpkins after Halloween and cooking them yourself. Pumpkins are abundant after Halloween. Ask your grocer before Halloween what he will do with the excess.

To cook the meat in the pumpkin, try one of these ideas. Cut the pumpkin in half and scrape out the seeds. Place the cut halves open side down on a cookie sheet and bake in a slow oven. Scrape out the meat and discard the shells. Another way is to cut the meat out and boil down to a pulp. Use the meat from either of these recipes in the same way as canned pumpkin.

Pumpkin Pancakes

1-1/2 CUP FLOUR
1-3/4 TSP. BAKING POWDER
3/4 TSP. CINNAMON
1/2 TSP. BAKING SODA
1/2 TSP. SALT
1/4 TSP. CLOVES
1-1/4 CUP BUTTERMILK OR SOUR MILK
3/4 CUP CANNED PUMPKIN
2 EGGS
2 T. BROWN SUGAR
1 T. OIL

Combine all of the ingredients and mix until smooth. Fry on a hot griddle or pan. Serve with maple syrup.

Pumpkin Bread

1 CUP CANNED PUMPKIN
1/4 CUP MAPLE SYRUP
1 EGG
2 T. VEGETABLE OIL
1 TSP. VANILLA EXTRACT
1-1/2 CUP FLOUR
1/2 CUP BROWN SUGAR
1/3 CUP RAISINS (OPTIONAL)
1 TSP. BAKING POWDER
1 TSP. BAKING SODA
1/4 TSP. GROUND CINNAMON
1/2 TSP. SALT
1/4 TSP. GROUND CLOVES
1/2 TSP. ALLSPICE

In a mixing bowl combine all of the dry ingredients. Add other ingredients and blend.

Do not over mix. Pour into greased and floured loaf pan, and bake for 50 minutes at 350°.

Roasted Pumpkin Seeds

Rinse seeds. Toss seeds with 2 T. vegetable oil and 1 T. salt. Spread the seeds on a cookie sheet. Bake in the oven 350° for 1/2 hour, stirring occasionally. Let cool—and eat! For variety, try a little onion salt or chili powder seasoning before baking.

Pumpkin Soup

> 6 CUPS RAW PUMPKIN
> 1 LARGE PEELED TOMATO
> 1 ONION, DICED
> 2 CUPS MILK
> 1 TSP. BROWN SUGAR
> 3 T. BUTTER
> SALT AND PEPPER TO TASTE

Combine pumpkin, tomato and onion in a pan and simmer until tender. Pour in a blender and mix. Add the rest of the ingredients and blend. Return the soup to the pan and heat 2 minutes.

FRUITS

Lemons

When I get bags of lemons from friends, I juice them all and freeze the juice in ice cube trays. Then I pop the cubes into baggies and keep them year round for whenever I need it for cooking or lemonade. One cube is the juice of about 1/2 lemon.

Apples

When my mom's apple tree is in season, we suddenly have lots of great apples. We eat the best of them, and store the rest by making applesauce (simply boil them down and mash with a fork), cobbler, apple butter, freezing pieces in plastic bags ready for pie at any time, and even drying them (thinly slice and lay on baking sheet overnight at 200°).

BERRIES

Growing your own berries is the best way to enjoy these lovely fruits. When a berry is vine ripened it is so much sweeter than any store bought version. If you cannot grow your own, visit a local farm that allows you to pick your own fruit. We visit a berry farm that is 40 miles away. Many question the cost savings factoring in the gas consumed in driving. The day is a fun outing for the family as we enjoy the fresh farm air together. The raspberries and strawberries that we picked were 75% less than the stores sell. We made jam and cobblers that lasted for months. Making jams are the best way to use up some extra fruits before they spoil. Frozen fruit pops, fruit leather, and fruit juice are also great uses for extra fruit. My easiest recipes for these are in the Some Great Recipes chapter.

Homemade Fruit Juice

Cook the fruit in a large kettle with very little water added. Drain the juice, and add one cup of sugar to each quart of juice. Boil, then skim any foam. Pour in bottles and seal with paraffin wax. This works with grape, cherry, apple, plum, and most fruits.

Cranberries

After Thanksgiving, fresh cranberries go on sale. Buy several bags of these to make into juice or jelly. They can be frozen for up to a year.

Cranberry Sauce

> 1 BAG CRANBERRIES
> 8 OZ. FROZEN CONCENTRATED APPLE JUICE

Simmer together for 5 minutes and refrigerate.

Dinner On Meeting Night

T HE CLOCK has struck five. You dash to your car and make your way to the freeway. You navigate the traffic. You hope your kids will be ready to jump into the car when you get there. All the while you are wondering if you will make it to the meeting on time, get the kids fed, and not get indigestion. Sound familiar? Anyone with a regular weeknight activity knows the scenario.

Too often the meal on these nights is from a fast food restaurant. The convenience is nice, but the cost can add to your indigestion. A meal made at home costs an average of $3 for a family of four. A fast food meal for 4 averages $12. Some quick math reveals that this weekly ritual can cost you $50 per month. These figures are based on 2 kids' meals and 2 budget adult meals at leading fast-food restaurants.

Be honest. Doesn't a home cooked meal sound better than the weekly fast-food feast? Fresh vegetables (and not just potatoes), tasty entrees, healthier ingredients, and less fat, sodium and preservatives. These facts, added to my financial motivations, lead me to find a better way.

I have come up with two ways to tame the meeting night frenzy. Both of these ways requires cooking in advance. If the thought of cooking once per month sends shivers down your spine, don't give up yet. There is an easy way to cook in advance on a busy schedule.

My first suggestion is for people who can congregate at home for a few minutes before the meeting. On a previous night that does not have a meeting scheduled, double the recipe for that night's dinner. Store it in the refrigerator (no more than three days). Chop lettuce and carrots for that night's salad (this is a quick vegetable), and store them in separate bags.

On meeting night, all you do is heat the meal and throw the salad in the bowl. It will take the same amount of time as driving through the fast food restaurant. And it will cost significantly less.

So what does the family do that can't get home before a meeting? On days like that, I pack a picnic dinner the night before. It can be the extra dinner from a doubled recipe earlier in the week, or something simple such as sandwiches, salad, fruit, and rolls or muffins. For drinks, I make a thermos of juice. All of this is packed the night before.

If you are going to be away from home most of the day of the meeting, take the meal with you. Put it in the refrigerator at your (or your spouse's) work. If that won't work, drop it at the meeting location earlier in the day during errands when you are nearby. Most churches and meeting buildings have refrigerators.

If neither of these are options for you, invest in a small cooler and freezer packs. There are even small refrigerators for the car that run off of the cigarette lighter. This may be the best choice for those really on the go.

You might say, "this can't be very miserly!" If the fast food meals cost you $50 per month, how long will it take to pay for the cooler? Not long, I figure.

The key to surviving meeting night with your sanity and wallet, is to plan ahead. In our house it saved us a great deal of money over the years. Even if I had the extra cash to go to fast food restaurants every week, I would rather see it go to a good cause rather than a fast-food company.

Birthdays, Holidays & Special Occasions

WHEN IT'S TIME for a special occasion, we tend to throw the budget out the window. We think things like, "Oh, it's their birthday," or "But it's Christmas!" I think we try to make ourselves feel better about not being creative at times like these.

Should we be sending the message that love and money are related? I have found that what people really want are your efforts and thoughts toward them. A simple party and homemade gifts mean more to me than extravagance. I think the same goes for our kids. A room full of toys is overwhelming. A few well-chosen items are better received.

So, how do I keep the gift and party madness from putting me in debt for months? First I plan what we are going to spend. I list all of the people that we usually buy gifts for (birthdays and holidays) for the entire year, and the parties that we usually throw (birthday, Christmas, Thanksgiving, monthly church potluck, etc.). Then we decide the maximum amount that we will spend on each person for each occasion. We then add up the year's total and divide by 12. This gives us the amount that we need to set aside each month in order to achieve those goals. If it's too much for our budget, we then scale back on certain events or gift giving, and stick to it.

Below are some ideas that I have used for birthdays, Christmas gifts, and dates with my husband. I hope they help your household.

BIRTHDAYS

I keep birthday parties as simple as possible. A homemade cake, a few close friends, and a local city park usually are adequate. What kids enjoy most is playing with their friends and family. If more is desired, you can add simple games such as bubble wands, charades, homemade piñata's (paper-mache around a balloon), potato rolling with a spoon, or catching water balloons. You also can cut the cake into animal shapes. A few simple recipes are in the chapter, Some Great Recipes. There are several books on cake shape ideas at the library.

Other party ideas are to sleep in the backyard in a tent with a few buddies. Or have a pizza party—where they make the pizzas. If you like to give gift bags to the guests, scale those down, too. Buy colored lunch sacks and let the kids decorate them with stickers and markers. Buy bulk candy or bulk tiny toys at warehouse clubs or party supply stores. Don't pay several dollars for each child's bag just because that's what is available at the local stores.

If you like to go on outings for the party, go to a local zoo and take the lunch and cake. Buying their food and cake will cost significantly more. Compare these figures;

Party Costs Comparison

Do it Yourself:

local zoo	$2.50 x 6 kids =	$15.00
picnic lunch	$1.50 x 6=	$ 9.00
Total party cost		$36.00

Prepackaged party:

local zoo	$2.50 x 6 kids =	$15.00
buying food at zoo	$9.00 x6 =	$54.00
Total party cost		$69.00

There are numerous books in the library on fun, inexpensive birthday party ideas. My favorite is *Birthday Parties for Children: How to Give Them, How to Survive Them* by Jean Marzollo. It is full of age appropriate party and game ideas that anyone can pull off.

I realize that as my kids become teens their taste will change, but for now this is good. Sometimes teens don't want parties anymore. Some would prefer to go to the movies with some friends, or go miniature golfing. A friend of mine has two teens. She tells them the budgeted amount for the party, and lets them decide if they want a small party, or use the money to take a friend to an amusement park or other outing.

There is no harm in limiting the size or expense of a birthday party. We don't get everything that we want as adults. We shouldn't give our children the message that they can have what they want—especially if we can't afford it. That could inspire them to later use credit to meet their impulses.

When you give a gift to another child for their party, I try to apply my miserly ways. I am not cheap in what I give, but I plan and watch for good prices. If I wait until the invitation arrives, I will have to run to the store and pay full price for some toy. One creative idea that a friend does is buy the wooden baking tool set (roller pin, small board, knife) when they are on sale during the "dollar days" events at her local grocery store. She buys several for future parties. When the event arrives, she makes some homemade scented play dough (see the chapter on Crafts For Kids) and wraps it with the baking set. This gift costs her $1.50. Another is to stock up on small toys when they are on sale and store until needed. Don't give cash. You'll give more than you would spend on a toy.

HOLIDAYS

Holiday celebrations should be run in the same manner. The focus should be on the friends and relatives, not the food and gifts. To scale down the cost of entertaining, try to change the type of party. Instead of serving dinner, serve dessert or have "tea." Or have an hors d'oeuvre party, with some inexpensive items. I usually serve Tortilla Roll Ups (see my recipe in the chapter Some Great Recipes) and they are well-received. There are many good cookbooks at the library that specialize in inexpensive hor d'oeuvre recipes. If you want to serve a dinner, make the main dish and let others bring the side dishes. Or make dishes with less meat in them, or meatless all together (try a vegetarian lasagna for example).

Table decorations can be homemade. Find a craft for the kids to make that will look nice on the table. They'll have fun and the guests will enjoy seeing their artwork. Read a book on napkin folding from the library. This free activity can make a beautiful table.

Gift ideas for adults can be tricky. But I still believe that the same principle that applies to children's gifts, applies to adults' gifts. What people want is thought and effort more than money. I try to make my gifts for friends and relatives. Here are a few of my favorite ideas:

- *Make a sachet from a small piece of fabric with a simple ribbon tie. Fill it with any of the following: rose petals, cotton balls with vanilla powder, cinnamon sticks with orange peels and cloves, lemon thyme and lemon verbena leaves, cornstarch with a few drops of potpourri oil, or lavender flowers.*
- *I enjoy baking my gifts. Some of my favorite gifts from the kitchen are Grandma's Spiced Nuts, Sponge Candy, and Orange-Chocolate Truffles (see Some Great Recipes for details).*
- *For Valentines Day, I make strawberry milkshakes with red food coloring, and bake heart-shaped pancakes or pizza.*
- *Save the seeds from your garden harvest and make simple seed packets out of paper for each seed type. Decorate the packet for a personal gift.*
- *Give a movie pass and a bag of special popcorn kernels.*

When a baked or homemade item is inappropriate, I try to buy something. I watch for sales, and store gifts for holidays. I try never to pay full price. Waiting to shop near the holiday only will cost more. Few things are on sale, and you'll be tempted to pick items you wouldn't normally.

SPECIAL OCCASIONS AND DATES

My husband and I need some time alone (as do most couples). We like to go on dates, but can't usually afford the combined cost of a sitter, dinner at a restaurant or movie theater tickets. So, we've come up with some cheaper alternatives that are as fun. Try one to see how it works for you.

INEXPEN$IVE DATE IDEAS

🐷 Go on a walk at sunset time. It's beautiful and relaxing.

🐷 Pick a handful of wildflowers for your partner.

🐷 Go for a bike ride.

🐷 Go rummage through a flea market.

🐷 Visit a local art gallery.

🐷 Go to a local bookstore's readings of poetry—or just browse.

🐷 Go star gazing. Many community colleges have free observatory nights.

🐷 Go on a free tour near you (winery, factory, etc.)

🐷 Take a picnic basket to a park (do it indoors and pretend, if it is rainy).

🐷 Go out for coffee and dessert instead of dinner.

🐷 Go to matinees versus nighttime shows— they are sometimes half price.

🐷 Some employers sell theater tickets at half price.

🐷 Go miniature golfing.

🐷 Use two-for-one coupons for restaurants.

🐷 When it's too cold to walk outdoors, walk in a mall.

🐷 Send the kids to someone's house for the night. Enjoy the silence.

The Baby

AFTER SHARING SOME TIPS on how to save money on baby necessities with my friend, she encouraged me to have a chapter on saving with babies. I tried to cover all of the areas that caused a squeeze on our pocket book when we had our babies.

DIAPERS

I won't rehash the old debate of cloth vs. paper, but rather will share my discoveries regarding cost. The debate over the environmental impact of disposable versus the air and water pollution caused by diaper services is an interesting one, if you choose to look into it.

After evaluating these issues, I compared the average cost of 100 newborn sized diapers.

Diaper service	*$43/mo.*
Disposable (name brand)	*$42/mo.*
Disposable (store brand)	*$21/mo.*
Cloth, do it yourself	*$20/mo.*

The only true saving is doing cloth diapers yourself. But it is a close finish with store-brand disposables right behind. For the cloth diapers, this figure is based on doing five loads of diapers per week. The energy cost of the washer and dryer is approximately $1 per load (see utilities chapter for how I figured that out), which equals $5 per week (or $20/month). I did not include the original cost of the cloth diapers. The off-brand disposable diapers are not bad, as I previously had believed. We have never had problems with the store-brand generic type. Many name-brand companies are selling their surplus to these generic distributors, who then package them.

BABY FOOD

Sometimes we believe that we need the products on the shelves to properly care for our babies.

The best way to save on food is to make your own. I found that if I mixed food that I had cooked for dinner (less the spices) with a few teaspoons of liquid in the blender, the food would be as good as store bought. This costs significantly less than a jar of pureed baby food.

There are many types of grinders available to make the food fine enough for the baby. If you don't have one, you can use your blender with good results. By adding a bit of water or milk to the food in the blender, you can get a smooth consistency. For added protein, add a bit of formula, if desired.

I did not want to be grinding food while trying to prepare a meal for the family. So I learned to make my babyfood in large portions. I stored it by filling ice cube trays with the food. I defrosted one square at a time, which was just the right size for a meal.

BABY WIPES

By making these yourself, you can save much money. I figure that a canister of homemade wipes costs 40 cents. Aside from the container of wipes on the changing table, we carry a canister of them in the car for messy faces and fingers. I also refill my travel pack with them, so I have some in my purse at all times.

> 1 ROLL STRONG AND THICK PAPER TOWEL
> (I PREFER VIVA'S ULTRA THICK, 50 COUNT)
> 2-1/4 CUP WATER
> 2 T. BABY SHAMPOO (FOR SENSITIVE SKIN USE MENNEN'S BABY BATH)
> 1 T. BABY OIL
> 1 WIPES CONTAINER (LARGE ROUND TYPE)

Cut the roll in half (making 2 smaller rolls). Use a large cutting knife and sharpen it right before cutting, and again during the cutting. Do not use a serrated edge knife. Set aside one half of the roll for another day. Remove the cardboard tube by grabbing the edge of it with a pair of pliers and twist as you pull. I recommended the VIVA Ultra 50 count because it fits perfectly in the container. If you use a larger roll, pull some of the paper out with the tube so that it will compress into the container. Combine the wet ingredients in the empty wipes container. Pour out 1 cup of the mixture. Place the roll in the wipes container (you may need to squeeze it a bit to fit). Pour the extra liquid on the paper to saturate the top half. Pull the wipes out through the center of the roll. To make pulling them out easier, cut some of the lid's small X opening away, making a wider hole in the center.

CLOTHES FOR KIDS

I spend about $350 per year on clothes for a family of four. The average American family spends more than $1000 per year. Our clothes look nice, without stains and tears. In order to spend this little, we must plan what our clothing needs will be and shop carefully. I figure how many outfits, dresses, dad's slacks, etc. we need each month or two. I then look for the best price on these items. If I stopped at a department store with my needs in mind, I would spend $100 each time.

If buying new clothes is a hardship, but you want your children to look nice, these are some good alternatives. I have found many great bargains at the "rerun" stores throughout our area. There are the big name places, such as Savers, Salvation Army, or Goodwill. Then there are the independent thrift stores in each city. Some of the wealthier neighborhoods might have a better class of clothing to offer. There also are the seasonal resale places (in our area there is one called Outrageous Outgrowns) where a few well-organized women set up a store for a few days where we can each sell our clothes, toys, etc. at the prices that we choose. Each of these offers some great clothes at great prices. Finding clothes may take some time, as the items come and go weekly.

If you prefer to buy new clothes, the best way is to watch sale flyers and stock up when prices are very low. One friend taught me to save even more by buying clothes one size too large, then loosely sewing the sleeve of a shirt into the cuff, and hemming the pants. When the kids grow, let out the hems.

Garage sales and local flea markets have a lot of variety. When you see one with children's clothes and toys, stop and investigate. Again, the wealthier the neighborhood, the better quality of items. I have found nice sweaters for a dime and good toys for 1/10th their value.

BABY-SITTING

The cost of baby-sitters can make going out a rare adventure. If a few moms form a baby-sitting co-op, everyone benefits. Most co-ops trade one hour coupons instead of money for watching each other's kids. To start one, ask your friends and neighbors if they are interested. It only takes a few moms to get one started. Make coupons for 1-hour sitting, and start each member with a pack of 10 (or whatever your group decides). Have a questionnaire for each member with basic questions: when she is not available, how does she feel about colds, does the family have pets, a pool, firearms, or other potential threats to a child's safety, and is she willing to do overnights. These forms can then be copied for each member, allowing the mom to pick who she prefers to do the sitting.

TOYS

The cost of toys can be high. We try to keep the cost down by shopping good quality resale shops. We also shop the sales at toy stores. Each store has a clearance bin with some treasures in it. We have found $25 games for $7. For a special item, we save and look for it on sale.

When the holidays are over, and the New Year's Eve dishes are still sitting in the sink, your checkbook is probably in shock. The last thing you probably want to think about is more toys. But now is actually the best time to think about it. Toys and gifts are going to be on sale. Many stores want to clear out the excess inventory left after the holidays. Buy that birthday gift for the kids that they didn't get for Christmas. Some of the best deals comes from the warehouse clubs clearing out the excess toys.

If there is no conceivable way that you can buy anymore right now, don't panic. Many items go on sale a few times throughout the year. These are great times to buy for birthdays, or even for the next Christmas.

When junior loses an important part of a toy, we tend to buy the whole toy to replace it. To save money, and toys, try contacting the manufacturer for that lost or broken piece. Most of the companies are very helpful, and understanding. Here is a list of some of the major manufacturers to help you save your toys:

Playskool *800-752-9755*
Milton Bradley *413-525-6411*
Fisher-Price *800-432-5437*
Lego Systems *800-422-5346*
Little Tykes *800-321-0183*
Brio *800-558-6863*
Hasbro *800-242-7276*
Mattel *800-524-8697*
Graco *800-345-4109*

TOY CONTAINERS

I was getting tired of all those little toys scattered on the floor, or sitting in a pile in the kids' rooms. So I began reusing many of our containers as storage bins for those little things. I use oatmeal boxes, large yogurt containers, large plastic containers that bulk pretzels come in, and boxes. No need to buy that expensive container box that the toy manufacturer wants you to believe you need.

The Cost of Working

WORKING IN AN EXPENSIVE AREA is very costly. This may seem confusing to some since most of us were raised to believe that if your expenses go up, so must your income in order to compensate. Losing half of our income, however, helped us realize that there were many hidden costs in a working person's lifestyle.

When I chose to stay at home with my children, we assumed we would have to move to a less expensive suburb to compensate for the 50% loss of income. But when I couldn't go through with the move, we were in a pickle. Same house. Same lifestyle. Half the money. Even though I wanted to be at home full-time, out of desperation I looked at working part-time. Soon I realized how much working had cost me. Many expenses had surprisingly disappeared after I quit.

Financial experts have calculated the cost of working at anywhere from $9 to $16 per hour. I was stunned when I learned this! That meant that if I took a job paying $10 per hour, I would only see $1 for every hour that I worked.

Here are the expenses that went into these experts' calculations:

- *child care*
- *taxes (local, federal, state)*
- *commuting fees (tolls, parking, etc.)*
- *gasoline and mileage*
- *car insurance (extra car, nicer car for the job, etc.)*
- *clothes (new clothes, cleaners, accessories, etc.)*

- *gifts for co-workers*
- *fast-food lunches and breakfasts*
- *convenience foods at home*
- *extra eating out*
- *occasional housekeeping help*
- *hair care*

Every person has a different cost of working. Some people have several children in daycare, while others have no children. Some commute many miles to work, others ride a bike. Some can wear casual clothes to work while others are required to dress in suits. Some pay more taxes than others. By using the list above, factor your cost of working.

After looking at my own experience, I soon realized that the experts' figures were accurate for me. I was spending $9–10 per hour for the privilege of working.

One area that I saw a change in our spending was work clothes. Working sometimes requires special clothes. If not special ones, you need more outfits to rotate in your wardrobe than you do if you're at home. Few people wear the same 5 outfits to work in rotation each week. We tire of something long before it is not useful. So, back to the department store we go. Then there is the cost of the accessories. For women, the cost of pantyhose alone is steep. And don't forget the high heels that need to match the outfits. And the earrings, etc. For men, the cost of suits or dress slacks is high.

Aside from clothes, there is the cost of transportation and parking to figure. Some need a nicer car than they would if not working. One that they can use for the transport of clients or co-workers. Some families might be able to eliminate one car if someone didn't work. The cost of wear on the car and tires, plus gasoline comes to 31¢ per mile (at the time of this writing). That's considerable when you see how many commuting miles you put on the car each day. Then there's the parking fees and added insurance for an extra car. In our area, they charge more if the car is used for commuting.

And then there is child care. Where I live the cost of child care runs from $350–700 per month per child. That's a lot of money. But I paid the $700 while I worked because I wanted the best for my child. But I still wanted to be with him and see how he was doing. Not because the care wasn't excellent, but because I wanted to know how he was. Perhaps we should add to the experts' list the cost of counseling from all of the worrying we do about our kids and the stress we encounter by working. I didn't want to do it anymore after 3-1/2 years. Even after the cost of working was taken out of my income, I still had some left for us to enjoy. But I would rather be poor and know how my kids are developing, than have more money and be working for the best child care and toys.

We must not forget the portion due to Uncle Sam when we work. And remember that the more we earn, the more they take. Most two income families have a higher tax bracket than a single-income family. If one parent stops working, the tax deductions from the other spouse's salary may fall into a lower tax bracket. This can add up to a substantial amount of money.

We must not overlook the savings we can achieve on the purchases that we need to make. I am speaking of gifts for relatives or co-workers, household items, appliances or even furniture. When we are working, we can't scour the sales and look for the best deals. We can't slowly acquire our Christmas and birthday gifts year round as we see a sale somewhere. I'm not saying that working folks don't shop around or look for good deals. I am saying that they may be less able to watch for sales or visit several stores before making their purchase. When I was working, I sometimes had to "settle" for what seemed like a good deal, because I had no time to go to several other stores to compare. Many people who work do make time for all of this shopping around, and they should be congratulated for their efforts. But they might be paying a higher price somewhere else, such as in a lack of time with family members or hiring household help since their free time is spent elsewhere.

The last area of working costs that many overlook is the additional food expenses that working people incur. A working parent is very busy and tired. They often forget or don't want to make homemade lunches for themselves, so they eat out. Even if it's cheap it will run $4–6 per meal. Most of us work 20 days per month, so lunches could cost you $180 per month. Then there's dinner to prepare when you get home. The working parent often relies on convenience meals or eating out because they don't want to cook from scratch, or there isn't enough time to wait for the food to cook. These conveniences cost up to six times more than a homemade meal costs.

Once I looked at these expenses that vanished when I quit, I decided to total them. Then I combined these costs with the ways I was going to reduce our spending, to see the overall savings of not working.

Here is a list of the areas in which we reduced our spending:

groceries	*$250*	*per month*
not eating out	*$125*	*per month*
clothes	*$ 75*	*per month*
haircuts	*$ 60*	*per month*
automobile	*$ 50*	*per month*
(gasoline & insurance)		
medical insurance	*$ 25*	*per month*
cleaning supplies	*$ 10*	*per month*
TOTAL REDUCED SPENDING	*$595*	*per month*

This savings amount, combined with the loss of the "cost of working" makes for a healthy reduction in expenses.

Total reduced spending (from above)	*$595*	*per month*
My cost of working	*$915*	*per month*
TOTAL SAVED BY NOT WORKING	*$1510*	*per month*

$1,510 per month = $18,120 per year!

What this figure means to me is that if I returned to work, even if only part-time work, I would lose the first $18,000 of that salary to added expenses.

Help for the Working Mom

IN PREACHING THE VALUE of not working, I don't want to overlook the working mom. Many women must truly work. They have squeezed every penny they can from the budget, but it isn't enough. They may have an unexpected emergency or other high expense that the budget cannot absorb. Or they might be a single-income parent. Some may not have any children and enjoy working, but need help with the budget. Whatever the reason, this chapter is dedicated to helping the working mom stretch her dollar.

As I discussed earlier, the area with the largest savings is groceries. This also is true for the working mom. After reviewing the eleven guidelines, I have summarized how she can apply them and make the best use of her limited time.

GROCERIES

She still can put a major dent in the food bill, but will need to approach shopping and cooking differently. Most of the eleven guidelines can apply to the working mom, but the following are the best use of time.

1) *Do your shopping and cooking once a month.*

You won't have the time to go to the three or more stores per week to get foods at the lowest prices. Since you can't take full advantage of the loss leaders at the local stores, buying in bulk is your next best option. Shop the good deals two to three times per month and buy enough for the month's meals. For example, buy chicken when it's on sale for 59¢ per pound. And buy enough for the month. Or better yet, go in with others and buy enough ground turkey or beef to get a low price from your butcher.

With all this bulk food, you should then set aside two to three days per month to cook. Prepare the month's meals and freeze them. The shopping can be done over two to three days, and the cooking in 1 day.

With this plan you will save money and time by:

- *bulk buying (lower costs)*
- *homemade "convenience" meals in the freezer (reduces eating out)*
- *less time each evening spent cooking and washing pots and pans*

2) If cooking monthly isn't an option

Plan menus around the items on sale at your local store. Don't go to the store and decide what you need. Grab the flyer at home and plan the menu around the loss leaders. This step alone saves quite a bit.

3) Stock up on sales

When your local store mails a coupon book, use it. Stock up on the things you regularly use. Go there only once each month and buy those things you use. Don't buy other things that you wouldn't normally buy, but are tempted by their low price. Buy enough to last you six weeks. That's when another coupon book comes out.

4) Don't eat out

Make your own sack lunch. Those cafeteria lunches add up. As I said earlier, I spent $180 per month when I thought I was eating cheap. Avoid the vending machines, even for a soft drink. They charge three times more than you can pay. Take a thermos of juice, or six-pack of soda and leave it in the office refrigerator. Don't grab coffee or breakfast at a restaurant or cafeteria on the way to work. Fill the coffee maker the night before and flip the switch on your way to the shower in the morning. Grab a banana and toast if you're late. You'll save.

CLOTHES

To combat the high cost of a work wardrobe, you must look at the styles that you wear, where you buy them, and how you clean them.

As for the styles that you wear, avoid the stylish fashions. Don't buy anything that can only be worn alone, such as a fancy shirt or patterned dress. Stick with classic designs and colors that can be mixed and matched, and that will still be in style five years from now. I buy neutral-colored shirts that can be worn with any neutral skirt or slacks. It can be combined with another neutral jacket or skirt for a completely different outfit. If I spent the same amount on a dress, I could only wear it once in awhile, as opposed to the several times with the mix and match approach. The same goes for shoes. Don't buy red shoes for the red dress. You can only wear them with that outfit. Buy neutral colors (brown, tan, navy, gray, black) and wear them with all the outfits. Remember, you aren't running for fashion queen. You're trying to keep your money for your family.

Pick fabric that can be hand or machine washed. The dry cleaners take a big chunk out of your budget. Buy lighter weight fabrics that can be worn in layers when it's colder, and alone when warm. For men, buy an extra pair of slacks when you buy the suit. They wear out at twice the rate as the jacket, and you won't be throwing out a jacket that's perfectly good.

For the underwear and pantyhose, buy in bulk from the manufacturers. Most have outlet stores in malls. Most offer catalogs. Many have frequent shopper cards where you get free purchases after a certain amount is spent. Buy their irregular or imperfect pairs to save even more. I have saved another 50% by buying irregulars. Wash pantyhose by hand and rinse in fabric softener to help them last longer.

Buy used clothing. I have seen many consignment shops or used clothing stores that specialize in office clothes. No clothes are accepted that are worn or stained. You can save 50% off what you'd pay for retail.

Watch for sales at the discount clothing stores such as Ross, Dress For Less, or Marshalls. Many stores clear out fashions or seasonal clothes at 40%–50% off. Stock up. You shouldn't be growing anymore, so you can buy for next year with confidence that it will fit. Check out their prices on socks and other accessories, too. They might be on sale.

Avoid the so-called sales at the big name department stores. The bigger name stores have inflated prices and then have 40–50% off "sales" to lure you in. Compare their prices to the discount department stores.

The Husband

WHEN TALKING with a few friends about their budgets, one had a great question... How do you get your husband committed? That's not meaning committed to an asylum, but committed to a budget and the miserly ways.

This proves to be one of the harder parts of the miserly lifestyle. If you are pinching the copper from each penny, but your husband eats out for lunch each day, you have a hole in the budget bag.

After the birth of our second child, I was too tired to shop. I sent my dear husband to the store with a list. He was not interested in my method of shopping at a few stores and only buying sale items. He went to one store and bought everything. He spent twice what we usually did for one week of groceries (the salsa and chips helped). I realized, then, that he needed to be convinced of the payoff in my method of shopping.

In order to get my husband to agree to the other spending changes that I wanted to try, I needed to convince him that those changes would be easy and profitable. Men tend to want to see numbers on paper to help them understand. Many men feel that all you're doing is saving a few cents here and there. As you know, it's much more than that.

The best thing I did to convince my husband was to annualize the savings that we could achieve. By reducing expenses and applying my guidelines to our groceries, I showed him that I could save $7,140 per year from our current budget. By quitting my job, I could reduce other hidden expenses by another $10,980 per year. By doing both (quitting and applying miserly ways), I was saving our family more than $18,000 per year. Ask him what he could do with an extra $18,000.

The other thing that impressed my husband was the first major purchase made with the savings I had accumulated. After two months of miserly shopping and cooking, I had set aside enough money to buy six oak dining room chairs. That spoke to him.

Another thing that helped convince him this was all well worth the trouble was when I explained that it doesn't take that much time. It takes about seven hours per week to apply the things that I have learned. Here is a breakdown of how that time is spent:

Hours Per Week To Be Miserly

Task	Time
shopping	2–1/2 hours
planning	1/2 hour
shopping extra stores	3/4 hour
(bread store, warehouse clubs, super sale somewhere)	
extra cooking	3 hours
(homemade versions of muffins, cookies, syrup, granola,	
relishes, snacks, etc.)	
	Total: 7 hours/wk

If all else fails, try to make a deal with him. Ask him how much he thinks he needs to spend each week (lunches, magazines, etc.). Then ask him if he would take that amount in cash and leave the rest to you. Then you can be a thrifty person in shopping, cooking, and other household areas and show him how much you saved (cash speaks loudest) at the end of two to three months. If he enjoys eating lunch out, ask him if he'd take a sack lunch to work instead. Show him how much his lunches out are costing the family. Promise him that you will make the lunch a tasty meal.

Another helpful agreement that stops major leaks in a budget is to make an agreement that neither of you will buy anything over $5 without consulting the other person. Before you drop your coffee cup, think about this idea for a moment. This policy doesn't apply to any "mad" money that you each get as an allowance. You can spend that where you like without anyone's opinion. It's those trips to the department stores or the mall that get us into spending trouble. It's that cute outfit in the catalog, or a nice kid selling stuff to raise money for a school. By having to discuss it, it gives you time to reflect on whether you really need it, and to compare the price to somewhere else. It also curbs impulse buying the manufacturers hope we will fall into.

Many husbands (like us wives) tend to have certain weak spots in which they spend freely. My husband's weak spot was books. He could drop $100 per month in books. He justifies it since they are reference or research books, not junk. I needed to help him find an alternative way to satisfy this urge or our financial ship was going to sink. We learned how the inter-library loan system worked. Your library can access almost any library in the US. We were amazed that you can check out any book you need with a free card. Even if the book is new, you can request it be purchased or borrowed from a library that just purchased it. We also discovered that we could rent movies, records and tapes for free. This helped plug that hole in the ship. Be creative with any trouble spots that your family has with money.

If all of these ideas still sound nuts, try writing down everything you spend for one month. Writing checks for everything helps in this endeavor. Then categorize what you spent (entertainment, food, subscriptions, clothes, household, hobbies, bank fees for overdraft charges, etc.) and figure the total for each category. See how much was wasted on trivia. Show your husband the damage. He might become a convert then.

Ten Ways To Get Kids To Save

W HILE SHOPPING, it is very easy to give in to a child's persistent whining about a toy or special food treat, especially when you are holding a toddler, a shopping list, and your diaper bag. It's easier to grab what is convenient or familiar and get out of the store as fast as possible.

These are the times where your miserly skills are tested severely. The best way to solve this weekly battle is to get your kids on your side. Get them to see the finances your way. Then you can reinforce what you've explained while shopping. Let me explain a bit better. If junior understands there is a limited amount of money to be spent at the store, then he will say, "Oh, yeah" when you remind him you can't afford that impulse item or more expensive brand of cereal.

It's harder to get them to understand that there is a limit to the green stuff. Especially when they see the cash machines spitting out money whenever we ask. My kids used to say, "What do you mean we don't have any more money. Just go to the bank machine."

Here are some tips that have helped my kids be involved:

1. Shop alone as often as possible

This is, of course, the ideal situation. You can compare as you need to, stop whenever you want, regardless of what toys are in front of you (why do you think those toys are at their eye level?). And, most importantly, you can think. But, reality is something different. Since I home school, my children are with me most of the time. During school hours, there may be fewer kids in your shopping cart. Try shopping then.

2. Explain that we have a limited amount of money, and that choices have to be made.

Explain the concept of a budget, and that plans have been made for all the money the family has. Use a pie chart with colors for each budget area. Exact numbers are not necessary to get the point across.

3. While at the store, explain what amount you plan to spend at this store.

If they are used to seeing you buy whatever you want when you go shopping, then they won't understand why they can't do the same. Let them see you put some of your things back when you realize you spent beyond the budget.

4. Give them the facts: "I can't afford it".

Who said they should have everything they want.

5. Ask them if they want to use their allowance to buy it.

When faced with the decision to use their own money, they quickly realize the value of money.

6. Use the opportunity to help them learn to make choices.

Explain that if we buy this brand of cereal with the fancy toy inside instead of the generic one, the difference will prevent us from doing something else (a movie rental, or an outing of same value). Let them make the choice, and you hold them to it.

7. For the very persistent (and young), let them pick only one item that isn't budgeted for.

All other wants have to be traded for that one, so that when you get to the cash register, they only have one item.

8. When you are away from the store, let them see or learn about other economic lifestyles.

Let them see you donate some of your income to help others. Explain how you planned for that donation in the budget.

9. If there is a certain item that they always ask for, show them how the system works.

Let them watch for sales and coupons in the grocery fliers and Sunday coupons. My son loves a certain brand of ice cream that is very expensive. I normally don't buy ice cream unless it's a great sale or I have a wonderful coupon. One day I found him on the floor going through the Sunday newspaper coupons. He found a great coupon for that brand of ice cream. He also saw that it was on sale at a local store. Eureka! At last he understands! (And he got the ice cream).

10. For those larger ticket items, I have found two ways to tame them.

First, I tell them to add the item to their Christmas or birthday list. I explain that most relatives enjoy getting a special item for them on a special occasion.

If they can't wait that long, I have them save their allowance for big ticket items. If it's expensive and special, I might match what they save.

Making a list of jobs for money around the home also is an incentive to earn the item faster. If they aren't interested in working for the item, then it must not be that important to them.

From these suggestions, I hope my kids will learn the value of money and patience. We will be constantly challenged. It's worth it to stick to your guns during those hard times. They need to learn that love should not be measured by money.

At mealtime, we need to teach our kids to eat what is available. This is my lifelong goal with my kids. I start slowly, introducing foods that I think they will like. Something that is an alternate version of a past favorite, such as tofu nuggets instead of chicken nuggets. I choose a soup that has something they like in it.

HOW TO SAVE WITH TEENAGERS

Someone said that my grocery spending goal was nice, but that I must not have any teenagers in the house. She was right, I don't have teenagers in the house. But I know many families that do, and who still only spend $50–60 per week on food. I asked them how they stay within their budgets.

These are some of their suggestions:

Food:

- *Watch what is being snacked on. Snack foods and teenagers can be a costly combination. Make your own muffins, breads, pizza, drinks, etc.*

- *If you can't make something very well (such as potato chips), stock up when they go on sale.*

- *Also, since bulk eating is usually an issue, practice bulk cooking.*

Name Brand Clothes:

- *Give them their allotted clothes money that would pay for good off-brand clothes on sale.*

- *Let them make up the difference for name brand clothes by using their allowance and job money.*

- *Show them how to shop for their name brand items at good resale, consignment and thrift shops.*

Miscellaneous Tips

H ERE ARE SOME TIPS on various topics that didn't fit into other chapters. They may be small matters, but they add up. Most have to do with daily life which, as we know, is where our money goes.

PHOTO DEVELOPING SERVICES

If you haven't looked, there can be a significant difference in the prices of photo developing and printing. Prices can range from $2 to $15 for a 35mm roll of film.

Some people think that the more expensive service produces the best picture quality. I wish this was true. The higher rates usually pay for fast service or a fancy name. The processing machines used by most developing houses are similar. Many stores send their film out to a central service. So it would be the same developer if you dropped the film off at warehouse clubs, your local camera shop, or at Safeway. The fascinating thing I learned is that many of these central houses are available directly to us. Two of these are very accessible and reasonable—York and Clark.

A consumer magazine did a survey of the most frequently used film developing companies, evaluating price, service, and quality. The best in all three categories were York and Clark. They charge about $2.25 for a roll of 35mm film, 24 exposure. I use these services and am always pleased. I get the pictures back in about a week. I can ask for faster service if I want to pay a small fee. They frequently send out mailers with an introductory price of 19¢. If you have not received one of their mailers, write to them at:

Chapter 23

Clark Color Labs
Box 96300
Washington D.C. 20090

York Photo Labs
Box 500000
Parkersburg, WV 26102

GAS

Gas is cheapest when you pump it yourself and buy at cash-only stations. I have found some cash-only stations that regularly charge 15¢ per gallon less than self-serve prices at other stations. They are able to charge less because they don't have the overhead expenses of credit cards. Some cash only stations are known for poor quality gas, but this is not true of all.

The average full-serve pump charges $1.50 per gallon (as of the writing of this book). The same station for self-serve charges $1.25 per gallon. Arco (a cash only station) often charges $1.09. Let's compare the savings using an average fill up of 12 gallons per week:

full serve @ $1.50 = $18/wk
self serve @ $1.25 = $15/wk
cash/self serve @ $1.09 = $13/wk

With a savings of $5 (between full serve and cash), we save $20 per month. Here are some other areas to save:

- *With frequent oil changes, tunes ups, and checking the air in the tires, you can save an additional 15% on mileage.*
- *If you have a pick-up truck, you can save 20% on your mileage by covering the tail end. The wind causes a drag as it scoops against the tail gate.*

FAST FOOD TOYS

Those little trips to the fast food places really add up. We think "Oh, it's just $5 for lunch for me and the kids, and they get a toy, too." I added those little trips and they were costing us $30 per month. I have since learned to plan ahead and pack a lunch.

But, I have yet to figure out how to make those cute little toys they offer in the kids meals. If there is a great toy the kids want, I drive through and buy the toy. If I only want a certain toy of a set that they are selling, I write to the local headquarters and ask for one. They usually do so for free.

MILK

There are a few ways to cut down on the cost of milk. If your household drinks a lot of the moo-juice, consider one of the following ideas.

The cheapest way to buy milk is to mix instant milk. The nonfat dry milk runs about $1.60 per gallon as opposed to the $2.40 per gallon of fresh milk. Most families can adapt and enjoy the savings. (Hint: The colder the mixed milk, the better it tastes). The nutrition is the same, and the lack of fat is a plus.

Some families buy whole milk then water it down. This makes the milk taste similar to 1% extra-light milk, and can reduce the cost of a gallon of milk by half. Try combining both ideas. Use a little instant dry milk in the watered down whole milk to add flavor.

If you live anywhere near a dairy, make the trip occasionally and stock up. You can freeze milk without problems.

BREAD MACHINES

Did you buy a bread machine because you think it will be cheaper in the long run? Well, you might be wrong. I have thought long and hard about the value of a bread machine. I owned one for three years and then it broke. I wanted another one, but couldn't afford the price tag. So, I researched the savings one would bring. I found that for most homes, it would not be a savings. The only case in which it might be a savings was for the multi-grain loaves of bread that included several different types of grains.

For my analysis, I compared the cost of bread at a day-old bread store or at a half-price sale, which is available to most people. I found that a store bought loaf of plain white, whole wheat, or buttermilk bread was the same cost as an equivalent loaf baked in a bread machine.

The cost of a multi-grain loaf of bread at a similar store was more expensive than a homemade loaf using the bread machine. I have however, been able to find 12 grain bread for 99¢ on sale every few months at a neighborhood store. At that price, homemade whole grain bread is more expensive. My analysis is below. I included the energy used by the machine for the mixing and heating stages, as well as the ingredients.

Without a good sale, the savings achieved by baking a multi-grain bread was worth the purchase of a bread machine. If the multi-grain loaf contained several types of grains (oats, wheat, wheat berries, sunflowers seeds, sesame seeds, etc.), a store bought multi-grain loaf of comparable size would cost about $2.50 where I live. A homemade loaf of equal size and grain usage would cost about $1.50.

I usually don't recommend buying a bread machine because most people don't use it much, or they intend to bake healthy whole grain bread but usually make easy white bread instead. If you, however, are disciplined in buying in bulk the ingredients needed to make a multi-grain bread, and will plan ahead and make it every time that you need a loaf, then you should buy a bread machine. If you can't do these things, and can take advantage of a sale such as the one I see often, the bread machine will be an unnecessary expense.

If you decide to buy one, make sure you have the feature that allows the bread to be air cooled after baking. Without this feature, your bread will become soggy unless removed from the oven within a few minutes after baking.

COFFEE

Coffee has become a trend for some, but is a necessity for others. I enjoy the brown liquid, and was a deep connoisseur for a long time. I went so far as to have the beans imported from Hawaii, since I felt these were the best tasting beans in the world. I think I have tried them all.

Some readers will be irritated that I even dedicated this much space and energy on coffee. One was especially bothered by the excessive mention of gourmet coffee stores. I do this because it is such a trend in the cities. They are fun places to gather with friends, and many folks, like me, love that Java bean. And, much of the time, their coffee does taste better than homemade. But I hope to offer some suggestions to make your homemade cup taste as good as theirs, and save you many pennies while doing it.

To cut down some of the costs of drinking coffee, I have tried these ideas—some of which may appeal to you; others may not:

- *If you think that your coffee tastes better at one of those trendy places, you're probably right. Your coffee maker at home does not get the water as hot as their store bought machines do. The extra heat gives the coffee more flavor. If you desire to get that cup of coffee as close to theirs as possible, try boiling water in a kettle and manually pouring the water over the grounds.*

- *To get the most flavor from your beans, don't grind them until you are about to brew. Even though coffee stays fresh for two to three weeks in the refrigerator, freeze the rest of the beans for optimum flavor. And remember that the finer the grind of coffee, the stronger the brew.*

- *If you brew coffee everyday, some people recommend reusing coffee grounds once by putting the used ones in the frig, then adding an equal amount of fresh grounds before brewing. This stretches the coffee expenses, but won't improve the flavor.*

- *Buy the expensive coffee filters and use them twice. Since they are made better, they can handle the wear. Better yet, buy the reusable type. They are made from either nylon or gold. They last for years and years (probably your lifetime), and will prove to be cheaper overall than paper filters. I bought a nylon one, and I have had it for 13 years. It is the dishwasher safe and can be rinsed after each use. The nylon does not affect the taste of the coffee.*

- *Don't buy a cup of coffee (or ground coffee) at the gourmet coffee shops. One lady called me and said she enjoyed her daily ritual of getting a cafe mocha and muffin at her gourmet coffee shop on the way to work. On the phone, we figured how much that was costing her each month—a whopping $65 per month. At home she could do it for $5 per month. When she wondered* *about the time she was "saving," we figured that to make it herself would take less time than stopping at the shop.*

As much as I like the trendy atmosphere of these places, you can save money and time by learning to make a premium cup. I love the taste of freshly brewed coffee, so I have learned to make a cup as strong as the shops do, and to make it at the time I want to drink it. If coffee sits on a warming plate for 15 minutes, it has already burned. Reheated coffee just doesn't taste that good to me, so I make it only when I want to drink it. Freeze leftover coffee in ice cube trays and use in iced coffee drinks.

When shopping for the best buy on beans, here is what I found:.

Cost of a Cup of Coffee

Type	Cost	Size	Unit Cost	Cost Per Cup
STORE BRAND	$3.89	13 oz.	30¢/oz.	6¢
NAME BRAND	$4.69	13 oz.	36¢/oz.	7¢
GOURMET BRAND				
at club store	$6.49	16 oz.	40¢/oz.	8¢
at grocery store	$7.99	16 oz.	50¢/oz.	10¢
at coffee store	$8.50	16 oz.	53¢/oz.	11¢
MAIL ORDER				
Hawaii	$9.00	11 oz.	82¢/oz.	16¢
GOURMET STORE				
brewed cup/plain				$1.25
brewed cup/mocha				$2.50

DECORATING

Decorating our homes can be limited when you live on a tight budget. A few resourceful women have shared some valuable ideas with me, and here are the best of them.

Curtains:

Get old curtains from a thrift store that are a good basic curtain, regardless of the print. Then find a bed sheet in the pattern you like. Shop sales or bedding outlet places and buy several of the sheets. I found my curtains were perfect for full sized sheets. Some curtains were the same size as 2 full-sized sheets sewn together, while some were one full-sized each. Take the curtain down, wash in cold water, and tumble or line dry for minimum shrinkage. Take out any bunching or pleating, but leave in the seams on the edges. The curtain should resemble a large rectangle. Sew the sheet around the edges of the curtain. Reapply any pleats then hang. Hem after hung. My six living room curtains cost $55 total.

Valance:

Take a 2x4 piece of wood, and cut the width of the window. Sew fabric of your choice into a tube (twice the length of the board) and bunch it around the board. Fix it to the top of the window opening, or nail to the wall.

Sofa Recovering:

If you have a fine sofa, but the material has had it from all those little feet and spilled bottles, here is a creative idea. Take some material that you like. For this, you can again use a sheet, or buy a heavier fabric at an upholstery fabric outlet store. They have the ends of the fabric rolls that furniture stores used. Attach the fabric to the existing seams with a staple gun. Remove the fabric in sections with a razor edge and use them as the pattern (add 2 inches to each side for tucking and mistakes). Our love seat cost me $60 to do myself. I was quoted $500 to have it done by someone else.

HAIR CARE

Most of us have to have our hair cut. So how can we save here? Many people go to the thrifty cutting places like Supercuts or Schroeders. Others have discovered the beauty colleges near them. They charge very little, and you are helping out a student.

Another idea is to find someone in your circle of friends and neighbors who does a fair job of cutting hair. If they are uncomfortable charging you for it, since they are probably unlicensed, try trading services. Exchange some haircuts for one sewing project, or other item you do well.

This savings can really add up. If a family of 4 gets a haircut on the average of every 6 weeks, they are spending the following each year:

trendy salon ($35/cut)	$1260/yr.
discount store ($9/cut)	$ 324/yr.
beauty college ($5/cut)	$ 180/yr.
trading services	$0/yr.
do it yourself	$0/yr.
let it grow	$0/yr.

We saved $60 per month by doing haircuts ourselves. The do-it-yourself option is easier than you think. Books can show you how to cut hair. There are even videotaped lessons available for sale. Practice on your kids first. Their hair grows fast and usually is messy from playing.

To clean hair, ask if you really need those expensive shampoos. Probably not. I have dry and curly hair. I have tried all of the hair care trends over the past decade, and have found I can get by with the cheaper brands just as well. I don't buy shampoo unless it's under a dollar. This happens more often than you think—just watch the ads.

COSMETICS

Cosmetics are expensive, causing many frugally-minded women to skip them altogether. There are, however, some ways to purchase good cosmetics at a discount, making them affordable for many. The first thing to explore are the generic or store-brand versions of famous cosmetics. Some come in a close second to the original. If store brands are not for you, the best way to purchase name brand cosmetics at a discount is through catalogs. Most of the large cosmetics manufacturers sell the remainder of a certain lot or color to surplus houses. These surplus products are sold for up to 90% off retail. Below are a few companies that offer free catalogs.

BEAUTIFUL VISIONS
P.O. BOX 9001
OAKDALE, NY 11769
(800) 645-1030
OFFERS PRODUCTS FROM L'OREAL, MAX FACTOR, REVLON, GIROGIO

BEAUTY BOUTIQUE
P.O. BOX 94519
CLEVELAND, OH 44101-4503
(216) 826-3008
OFFERS PRODUCTS FROM VARIOUS NAME BRAND COSMETICS MANUFACTURERS

ESSENTIAL PRODUCTS COMPANY, INC.
90 WATER STREET
NEW YORK, NY 10005
(212) 344-4288
OFFERS COPIES OF NAME BRAND PERFUMES

CLASSIQUE PERFUMES
139-01 ARCHER AVENUE
JAMAICA, NY 11435
(718) 657-8200
OFFERS COPIES OF NAME BRAND PERFUMES

CREDIT CARDS

This is one of the first problems people encounter when they get their first job. Someone offers them their first Visa or MasterCard and they are ecstatic. Until the first bill arrives.

Most people have several credit cards—Visa or MasterCard, a department store card and gas cards. In California, the average household credit card balance is $3900. And one in seven card holders says they are "in over their heads." Credit cards only are good for either 1) the convenience of paying when out of cash (but you need to pay the bill in full when it arrives) or 2) a true emergency. But most people (an astounding 75%) don't pay off the balance each month. And most consider an emergency as less than life threatening.

Don't rush out and cut up the cards. Sometimes they are necessary (like renting a car or hotel reservations). Instead, control your spending. See what you can afford (that means making a budget) and live within your means. If you are using credit cards regularly, then you are outside of your budget. Put the cards away in a safe place. Don't carry them with you (unless you travel). Regard them as emergency tools only. Most situations can allow you to go home and get the card and come back.

You must get rid of the debt as quickly as possible. If it takes a few years, do not despair. It's those small yet faithful steps that will get you to your goal of financial freedom. There are several steps that you can take to rid you of your debt faster.

First:

Get rid of the high-interest rate cards. Keep only one multi-purpose credit card and make it one with no annual fee and a 25-day grace period (no interest is charged from the date of purchase to the due date of the bill). These require that you pay the balance off each month to avoid high interest fees.

For help on how to get out of debt, write to Bankcard Holders of America and ask for the Debt Zapper plan (524 Branch Drive, Salem, VA 24153) or call (540) 389-5445. Another resource for getting out of debt is the National Center for Financial Education (P.O. Box 3914, San Diego, CA 92163). Ask for their free pamphlets "Fifteen Steps to Reduce Indebtedness" and "Dealing With Your Creditors."

Second:

Consolidate the bills to the lowest interest rate available. This may be the one credit card you have, or it may be a loan from your credit union or savings and loan. For a list of low-interest rate credit cards, write to Bankcard Holders of America at the address listed above. For $4, they offer a list of credit cards with the lowest fees and interest rates. Another resource is the RAM Research Corp. which offers a monthly newsletter which reviews credit card rates. You can get the latest issue for $5 (CardTrak, P.O. Box 1700, Frederick, MD 21702 (800) 344-7714).

Faithfully pay as much as you can each month—or more. Some people consolidate their loans and then refinance their homes so that their overall monthly payments are lower. This is okay if you already were going to refinance the home due to lower interest rates (it is recommended that the loan be at least 2 points lower to be worth the cost of refinancing). Sometimes this new lower total payment is deceptive. Even though the combined payments are lower, the overall debt may now be higher, since you added the high expense of refinancing (points, fees, etc.)

Third:

If you are "over your head," turn to a professional for help. There are credit counseling agencies everywhere. For a referral to a credit counselor near you, call The National Foundation for Consumer Credit at (800) 388-2227. You also can look in the yellow pages under Credit Counseling for more local listings.

VACATIONS

Plan ahead for the trip, and save wherever you can. If you only can save $500, then don't take a $900 vacation. Live with what you have. Save what you didn't spend on groceries, send in for rebates, do some baby-sitting or other odd jobs. It doesn't matter how small the money is. Stick it away in a savings account. I put as little as $2 in there. But I am faithful about putting whatever I could. Last year, at the end of 9 months, I had $700.

To keep the cost down for a vacation, don't use your credit cards. Unless you plan on paying the entire balance off by the time the bill arrives, you could be adding 18% to the cost of the trip (that's the average finance charge). If you decided to charge the trip and pay off later, instead of saving for the trip first, you could end up adding hundreds of dollars to the cost of the trip.

Eating in restaurants is a drain on the vacation cash. I try to eat in the room as often as possible, and save the cash for the fun outings. I get a small refrigerator in the motel room, and keep food in it. Then we have cereal in the morning, sandwiches at lunch, and a frozen meal for dinner (if there is a microwave in the room). Since I can't cook a meal from scratch, a frozen dinner is the next best bargain. A frozen dinner costs 3 times less than eating out. Also, many hotels offer a free family happy hour with hors d'oeuvres. These sometimes can be a meal.

What you pay for a room can vary greatly, so you must search out the best deals. Many hotels offer special rates on surplus rooms. Not all rooms are booked at all times, and these are the discounted rooms. But you have to ask if they have this type of discount. If you book a few months in advance it helps to get these rooms. If you are a member of a travel club, such as AAA, you also can get a substantial discount. Again, you have to ask if they have this discount. These two discounts saved us $150 on our last trip.

Other housing ideas come from those who exchange homes. There are several home exchange networks that can link you to another in need of a bargain vacation. These companies usually charge a fee for the service (but it can't be more than a hotel would be). Here are two that I know of:

INTERNATIONAL HOME EXCHANGE
P.O. BOX 3975
SAN FRANCISCO, CA 94119

VACATION EXCHANGE CLUB, INC.
12006 111TH AVE., UNIT 12
YOUNGTOWN, AZ 85363

There are other discounts available on travel arrangements. Our local warehouse club offers 5% cash back on any airline or Amtrak ticket purchase done through them. This means that you can find the best bargain and then get another 5% back. Several grocery stores also offer discounts on airline tickets with a certain amount of grocery receipt totals. This can be profitable for you only if you were already going to spend that amount at that store.

Don't turn your nose at the expensive airlines just because you need to save money. I learned of a special that one of the most expensive airlines offered by calling just to see what their prices were. It turned out their fare was less than any of the best deals on any other airline. These deals aren't advertised—you have to ask.

When making an airline reservation, pay as soon as possible. The prices can (and do) go up. But don't be in such a hurry to get the ticket that you make a mistake in the travel plans. Any changes will be charged a penalty. Ask if any discounts apply, such as staying on a Saturday night.

The use of credit cards is best when purchasing travel arrangements (airline, train or package deals). Many credit card companies offer insurance for yourself, your luggage, and even canceled trips. Check with your card carrier. But make sure you can pay the balance off when you return.

If you are going to be gone a long time, you will need to park your car somewhere (unless you can get someone to drop you off and pick you up). Here are your options:

- *Have a shuttle pick you up—$12 per person each way*
- *Park in the airport's long term parking—$8 per day*
- *Stay overnight in a motel nearby—free parking (they usually offer low rates and free shuttle to and from the airport)*

Car rental rates are as varied as there are companies. There always is a deal. Full price should not be in your contract. Get what you need (size, air-conditioning, etc.) and then review your options. Certain days of the week are cheaper. Returning at certain locations and days can be cheaper. Filling up the tank as close to the return location will be cheaper than paying them to fill it up.

Check what kind of insurance your insurance company offers on rental cars. Some cover you for injury as well as damage to the car. Adding any more insurance could be a waste of your money. But check the definition of the offered insurance. Some rental companies are combining theft with collision. If you decline, the theft of the car could be your responsibility.

TOOLS AND APPLIANCES

Many Americans have gadgets for this function and that. And many of these items only are used two to three times per year. Try going in with a neighbor or relative on a tool or piece of equipment that will be seldom used. Or, better yet, borrow it if you can. This applies to items like canning equipment, spray painters, fruit pickers, special ladders, etc.

If you think that you will use a tool two to three times in a year, then start shopping at garage sales. I got a great belt sander for just $20 (retail $50).

When those large appliances break, such as a washer or dryer, look at repairing versus buying a new refurbished one. Most larger items cost no more than $99. That's close to the cost of the labor alone in a repair job. Most local newspapers list companies that buy and sell used appliances.

If it's truly ready for the dump, don't pay someone else to take it away. Call one of the refurbishing companies and see if they can take it at no charge. They will use it for the parts they pull from it.

PAINT, VARNISH, CEMENT, ETC.

By looking around (not in dumpsters or garbage piles), I have been able to obtain paint, cement stones for my garden, and drywall for our house project for free. Much of what we throw out is not garbage, but rather surplus. Usually it's something we don't want to store.

As my mom used to say, "You won't know until you ask." Well, she was right. Whenever I see construction taking place near my home, I wait until they are done. Then I ask what they will do with the leftover wood, cement or paint. If it is a small job, the workers are usually glad to give it to you. They would have to go to the dump and pay to dispose of it otherwise.

There was some repair being done to the sidewalk in front of our home. Watching it proved to be educational and fun for the kids. When they were done, they were going to throw out the excess cement. We brought pans and buckets and had them pour it in there. We made hand prints and stuck shells and wrote in them. We have some cute garden stones that cost us nothing. I have seen stepping stone kits in catalogs for $26 that do the exact thing we accomplished.

This is how we got the paint for the outside of our garage. Some painters were finishing a painting job at a house nearby and had excess paint when the job was done. They were going to discard it so they let us have the excess paint for free.

One person recommended the local recycling center to pick up half - used cans of varnish, paint remover, etc. It is free for the taking. I personally am not comfortable with this plan. We don't know how old the containers are, or if chemicals have been mixed together.

FURNITURE

Aside from bargain hunting at garage sales and watching advertisements, furniture can be an expensive addition to the household. One family I know builds their own furniture—for free. They find furniture manufacturers or staircase makers, and take the scraps of wood left from their projects. Usually the wood is given for free, as long as they pick it up. My friends' latest project is an armoire entertainment center. It is made of solid oak scraps, obtained for free. The total cost was less than $20 for hinges and supplies.

If you do need to purchase furniture, don't be afraid to negotiate the price. Do some research on prices at other stores, and show the ads to the store. Make sure items are exactly the same item. Tell the salesperson what you can afford, and be sincere. This tactic got us $4000 taken off of the price of a car that we purchased. If you have any delays in the arrival of your order, don't be shy to negotiate upgrades to compensate for your inconvenience.

LEGAL ADVICE

Sometimes we have some legal questions about something we are doing, but we don't want to pay $100 per hour for the help. I'm not talking about when you are in an accident or being sued. I'm talking about that freelancing job you may want to look into, but don't know what to charge or if you need a contract. Or that magazine article you want to sell, but can't understand the contract they sent you.

There are a few organizations to help you for a small (or no) fee for 30 minutes of advice. One is called SCOPE and is manned by small business veterans that are happy to answer your questions about what to charge on a freelance job, or how to start that small business in your garage. Another I found was the Lawyers for the Arts. Here in California, they are called the California Lawyers for the Arts. They offer 30 minutes of legal advice related to the arts (literary, performing, film, etc.) for a minimal fee. Most chambers of commerce can direct you to these services in your area.

CHECK CHARGES AND BANK FEES

Most of us write checks and have to pay for them. Theoretically we can write a check on toilet paper, but each banking corporation has the right to refuse processing this form of "promissory note." Banks offer to sell you checks, but at a premium. We can go directly to the check manufacturers and save about half of what a bank would charge. The best deals come from Current (800-426-0822) and Checks In The Mail (800-733-4443). The first set of 200 checks is usually $4.95, and future orders are $6.95 (these are for plain checks). I have used Current for many years and know I have saved enough for a weekend vacation from this one activity.

For most of us, bank fees are a necessary evil. Lately, the banks want to charge for everything, and then some. I am charged if I go inside the bank to a teller window instead of using the ATM. Other banks charge for using the ATM as well. There are some ways to lower the bank fees. Ask your bank what services it gives discounts for. Our bank offers a $1 discount per month for each of these: payroll direct deposit, ATM use only, canceled checks on file at the bank. I also can get the entire monthly fee waived if I keep a certain minimum in the account all month. Sometimes a savings account may be more cost effective, if you don't use checks often and can conduct business with cash from the savings account. Credit unions are sometimes cheaper if you can join one.

LONG DISTANCE PHONE CARRIERS

There are so many long distance carriers that it can be confusing. Many of us don't switch because we don't understand who offers a better deal. The best deal will differ from home to home. A leading carrier that many friends claimed the cheapest was not the cheapest for my family. Our calling habits, times and locations were different than many homes. To do an accurate comparison, write down your calling habits. Are most calls to one area? Do you call at certain times of the day or week? With these needs in mind, call around and get quotes. Below are some of the carriers that I reviewed. There are far more small carriers available than I have listed.

AT&T ....*(800) 222-0300*
MCI ....*(800) 333-4000*
US Sprint ....*(800) 877-4000*
Lifeline-Amerivision ....*(800) 800-7550*
   (offers 10% of your total bill to charity of your choice)
Excel ....*(800) 875-9235*

To help you wade through a few of the carrier rates, a group called TRAC has compiled a listing of long distance rates. For a copy, send $5 with a SASE to Box 27279, Washington D.C. 20005.

SEASONAL SAVINGS

Almost everything that we need for our homes goes on sale at some time during the year. On the next two pages is a chart of when things typically go on sale. Your area may vary as to what sells at what time of year, but there should be some similarity. Modify the chart for yourself as you see variations.

SEASONAL SAVINGS CHART

Month/Sale	Clothes	Linens	Appliances
JANUARY-FEBRUARY			
WHITE SALE	men's shirts	towels	stock clearance
PRESIDENT DAY SALE		linens	clothes dryer
		sheets	used cars
			water heaters
MARCH			
END OF WINTER SALE	coats		TV
PRE-SPRING SALE	clothing for all		washing machines
	shoes		
APRIL-MAY			
AFTER EASTER SALE	dresses	towels	TV
PRE-SUMMER SALE	suits		tires
MOTHER'S DAY SALE	coats		
MEMORIAL DAY SALE	summer clothes		
JUNE-JULY			
FATHER'S DAY SALE	summer clothes		air conditioner
END OF SCHOOL SALE	shoes		
AFTER JULY 4 SALE			
AUGUST-SEPTEMBER			
END OF SUMMER SALE	summer clothes		
PRE-FALL SALE	fall clothes		
LABOR DAY SALE	school clothes		
	swimwear		
OCTOBER			
			cars from dealerships
			(buy close to last day
			of month for best deal)
NOVEMBER			
	men's shirts		water heaters
DECEMBER	(NOT A GOOD TIME TO BUY ANYTHING, UNTIL DECEMBER 26)		

Household	Furniture	Gifts	Groceries
weatherizing	clearance	Christmas	meats
treatments		wrap and	(turkey, ham)
art supplies		ornaments	baking items
bicycles		toys, etc.	
books			
curtains			
ski equipment			artichokes
housewares			
outdoor furniture		gift items	artichokes
paint			dairy products
tools			ham
garden supplies			eggs
summer sports			chicken
equipment			
school supplies	most furniture	gift items	dairy products
outdoor furniture			fresh fish
building materials			barbecue foods
			limes & lemons
school supplies	seasonal items	season passes	fresh fish
garden supplies			lamb
outdoor furniture			canned goods
rugs and carpets			
bicycles			
car batteries & mufflers			
summer sports equipment			
home improvement supplies			
houses are cheaper			

Medical Expenses

MEDICINE HAS become a big business, and we need to start learning how to play the game. It used to be that if you were sick, you saw a doctor. Now it's who you see, what services are provided and at what rate. Let's learn a few tricks to help reduce the expenses of illness. Please remember that the advice I share is lay advice, and should never be substituted for any professional health care advice.

MEDICAL INSURANCE

Many people make a superficial decision about which insurance carrier to pay. Some decide because they prefer the ease of a co-payment rather than submitting an insurance bill for refund. Our decision for our care should go beyond convenience. We should look at the type of care we'll receive, as well as the annual costs between carriers.

The first thing to remember is that you need insurance. Many families I know don't have it because they are mostly healthy or they can't afford it. One accident will wipe them out, or have them at other people's door asking for financial help in their tragedy. Another reason to carry it is that you will always be treated better if you have the insurance. Many doctors and hospitals won't provide care, or will but with less quality and attention than paying patients.

When I shop for insurance, the first thing I consider is the type of care I want. Is it important to me to have a doctor that I know and that I can always see each time I need to? Will I get the best testing done for a problem I encounter? Can I go where I think I need to? The answers to these will direct you to the type of carrier you should choose. An HMO (Health Maintenance Organization) will provide you with "managed" care. This means that they decide when you need further tests and they get to decide who does them. Some HMOs are more controlling than others, not allowing you to see the doctor of your choice. Some allow you to select the doctor of your choice, but then require that you stay within his/her clinic for all other medical needs. The thing to remember about this type of insurance carrier is that the more control they have over your care, the lower your medical premium will be. This is because they get to decide what care you get, and they save money when they provide less care.

When you decide what the right type of insurance is for you and your family, you should start doing some comparative shopping. The most accessible and the cheapest place for insurance is through your employer or your spouse's employer.

If you have no employer policy available, look at any professional groups that you belong to, your college's alumni association, your automobile insurance carrier, or any school you may be attending. Buying a policy as an individual will cost you 15–40% more than with a group. There also are companies that sell directly to individuals, such as Blue Cross or Blue Shield. There are groups of people who form their own insurance group by pooling their money. The families accepted must all adhere to certain lifestyles and health requirements (such as no smoking, drugs, etc.) to participate. These only cover the high expenses such as hospitalization and surgery, and not regular doctor appointments.

When you purchase medical insurance, estimate what your medical needs will be during the next year. List what you needed last year. Then consider things such as the types of hospital services you may need, surgeries, prescriptions, ambulance, well baby care, maternity, physical therapy, out of town coverage, chronic illness coverage, and any annual cap on what you will spend. Then factor in the potential carrier's portion. Below is our comparison of some carriers we evaluated. By doing this sort of evaluation, we saved $300 per year.

Expenses per Year	Carrier A	Carrier B	Carrier C
PREMIUM (family of 4)	500	700	1000
DEDUCTIBLE	200	0	0
DOCTOR'S VISITS:			
2 kids annual exam	30*	0	0
5 unplanned visits	45*	25**	25**
EMERGENCY (stitches, etc.)	75*	25***	25***
CHIROPRACTOR (average 6 per year)	60*	300	150***
MEDICATIONS (some won't cover certain drugs)	20	100	100
ANNUAL COST	$930	$1150	$1300

*20% is our portion
**$5 co-payment per visit
*** $25 co-payment per visit

Once you have selected a carrier, find out about their policy on visits to urgent care facilities and emergency rooms. One type of service might be covered at a very different rate than the other. Also, some carriers restrict the coverage of certain types of visits to urgent care facilities and emergency rooms, and might even refuse to pay.

A few more things to remember when choosing insurance:

- *Don't always assume that cheap is better. Check out the reputation of the carrier. Make sure that the company that you pick has a high rating by Best Insurance Reports (available in most libraries).*

- *Don't under-insure you or your family. Make sure you will be covered for major things. When choosing life insurance, make sure your family is left with enough to pay the mortgage. Find out if your spouse plans to work after your death. If he/she does plan to work, how long he/she will need before returning to work. Add that annual need in.*

- *Consider your need (or lack of need) for accidental death insurance. You are more likely to get disabled than to die from an accident. Unless of course you are very reckless. Also, heart attacks are not considered an accident.*

- *Pay as high a deductible as you can. You want to only pay for coverage of losses that you cannot afford. The higher the deductible, the lower the payments.*

HOSPITALS

Most people assume that a doctor or hospital bill is a fixed fee. In many cases it is, but not always. Many doctors are very understanding and will accept whatever the insurance company will cover combined with whatever you are able to pay. Many large bills can be negotiated, especially if the hospital is in a lower income area. These hospitals have many customers who just can't pay for their visit, so the hospital has to write off the cost. If a customer can pay, but needs to make small payments, they usually cooperate to get their money.

My husband had to spend three days in intensive care at a hospital in a lower income part of a city. When all of the various bills arrived, there were 12 in all. We could only afford to pay each $10 per month. All of them (except the hospital) were willing to accept these terms, and none ever charged interest.

On a separate trip to a hospital a few years later, we landed in a wealthier part of town. This 4-hour hospital stay cost more than our 3 day visit to intensive care at the other hospital. This hospital did not want to accept payments. Instead they offered us a 20% discount if we paid by the end of that month. That added up to a large savings, and was worth doing what we had to in order to pay.

Don't be afraid to contest the amount that the insurance company decides to cover. There are humans with tender hearts working at these companies. I have had medications and procedures covered that normally would not, because I wrote a sincere and explanatory letter regarding the situation. Send supporting documents, such as a doctor's letter, if you can.

DOCTOR BILLS

When you finally use the insurance carrier, find ways to reduce the expense of the bill. Use their preferred doctors and save 40%. Ask the carrier how else you can reduce your part of the bill. Some doctors will write off your portion of the bill if you show financial need.

Use the phone as often as possible instead of making an appointment. Many doctors will advise you and even prescribe something over the phone. You save $50 by letting your fingers do the walking.

Check out what your local county board of health has to offer. Many offer immunizations for children for free or for a minimal fee of $5. A visit to the doctor for the same service runs $75.

MEDICATIONS

Another area of savings is generic versions of prescription drugs. This can save you 30–80% compared to the cost of name brand drugs. I have seen a drop from $20 to $100 for one prescription, just due to the generic version of the identical drug. Even many over-the-counter drugs can have a large variance between a name-brand and a generic version. The best way to reduce the cost of drugs is to use generic as often as possible, and then to shop around. Many stores and warehouse clubs have varying rates for store-brand versions of drugs.

I have heard of some people who won't buy generic brands, insisting that only name brands be purchased. Many feel the inventor of that item needs to be encouraged to continue inventing new products. These shoppers feel if we buy the generic version, the inventors cannot afford to continue their good work. We must remember that no one stole the recipe for the generic version. Most generic drug formulas only come on the market after the original patent has expired. The original manufacturer holds this patent for many years and makes a great deal of profit from the formula before it is made public. Much of the original research was done independently, and then sold to a major manufacturer. So many of the big name advertisers didn't invent it after all. That manufacturer also sells much of its original product to the generic companies to be resold as a generic brand.

Don't overlook mail-order pharmacies, such as Medi-Mail (800) 331-1458, Action Mail Order (800) 452-1976, and America's Pharmacy (800) 247-1003. These are great for medications that you use regularly. They can give a good discount, up to 60% off name brand prescriptions. If you have access to the AARP (American Association of Retired Persons), they have arranged good pricing as well. Contact their pharmacy for details at (800) 456-2277.

For colds, I don't buy the all-in-one remedies that are advertised so heavily. You end up taking stuff that you don't need and paying for the convenience of having them combined. A bottle of decongestant with acetaminophen added will cost 20–30% more than if you buy them separately. Instead, know the ingredients and buy those generically. Keep several separate bottles in the cabinet—one for each type of medication. I keep a piece of paper taped to the inside of the medicine cabinet that tells me what each ingredient is meant to help. When I have a certain symptom, I take just that drug. Some people like the hot flu medication drink that is packaged for your convenience. Instead take what you need (fever reducer, decongestant, etc) and have a hot cup of herb tea or hot water with lemon juice and honey. The same effect will be achieved and cost alot less. Below is the list that is taped to my cabinet, in hopes it will help you.

Generic Names and Purposes for Cold Medications

Name	Purpose
dextromethorphan	for dry cough/ cough suppressant
guaifenesin	for gooey cough/expectorant
pseudoephedrine	decongestant
phenylpropanolamine	decongestant
ephedrine	decongestant
chlorpheniramine	antihistamine
diphenhydramine	antihistamine

It's important to know what you need. You can complicate your problems by using the wrong drug. For example, if you have a gooey cough, using a cough suppressant isn't a good idea. Ask your doctor or pharmacist before you self-medicate to be sure you're choosing the right medicine.

When shopping for vitamins, the same guidelines apply. Know what elements you need and shop around for the best generic price. Don't forget to check the expiration dates as well. To know if you are getting a good manufacturer of the tablet, try this quick test. Drop a tablet in a few teaspoons of any kind of vinegar (to simulate stomach acid) and leave it for 45 minutes (you can stir it once in a while to simulate stomach churning). It should break apart or dissolve by the end of the experiment. If it doesn't, then the manufacturer packs it too tightly or adds too many fillers and it passes through you unabsorbed. I tested all of my vitamins and found one of mine that didn't dissolve. All the time that I took them, I wasn't getting any benefit from them. I wrote to the manufacturer and received a full refund. If you would like to know which brands of multi-vitamins are more complete, check the library for recent articles that review the most popular brand of vitamins. One newsletter with a good vitamin review is the Nutrition Action Healthletter written by the Center For Science In The Public Interest, 1875 Connecticut Ave, NW, Suite 300, Washington D.C. 20009-5728, (800) 237-4874.

With any medication you buy compare the unit price (the cost per milliliter or milligram). Sometimes it's cheaper to take two capsules of a lesser dose than to take one of a larger dose. This is particularly true of aspirins and other pain killers. Again, you are paying for the convenience of someone combining doses for you.

DENTAL EXPENSES

As much as I hate to admit it, the dentists are right. Prevention is the best way. By brushing after meals, flossing, and getting regular cleanings, we prevent plaque from eating away the enamel and causing expensive cavities or root canals. I know this because I did not practice good dental care until a few years ago. And now I am paying for it. I don't mean that I was not brushing and flossing. I was doing both, but either at the wrong times or not frequent enough. Most of us eat between meals without brushing. And many of us do not floss every night. When I learned that 35% of all gum disease and tooth loss comes from plaque destroying teeth, I took notice. A root canal can cost $250 per tooth. You can buy alot of dental floss and brushes for that. You can also save yourself some gum and enamel damage by using the right kind of brush and by brushing correctly. Listen to your dentist as they show you the correct way.

Toothpaste is worth investigating. You don't need the big name brand tubes to have healthier teeth. You can also use less paste than the television commercials suggest. That will save a few cents with each brushing. When I grew up overseas, we could not get toothpaste. We could order tooth powder, but when we ran out, we used the healthy standby—baking soda. You can mix it with cinnamon, mint extract, or a flavored fluoride liquid to enhance the flavor. This is healthy for the teeth and gums and very cheap.

The whole idea of brushing is to keep the foods (particularly sugar) off of the teeth so plaque isn't encouraged to grow. So, if you brush, don't snack right after. When you brush in the morning, do it after breakfast. The same principle applies to our kids. Don't let them snack or drink juice or milk all day. The constant food and sugars in the liquids are feeding the plaque. After they eat a meal, brush their teeth and snack on non-sugar items such as vegetables and water. Make sure they go to bed with clean teeth and no bottles or cups of juice or milk. All of this may sound excessive, but it is the only way to assure healthy teeth.

To save on the professional cleanings, try a local dental school or community college. They charge as much as 75% less than a private dentist. Another source of savings would be to check with local universities. Some have a dental program and offer low cost appointments by students in training. These students always are supervised by certified dentists. The cost of an average visit is 50% less than a similar visit to a dentist in private practice. If you cannot afford much at all, check with your local county health department. Many offer low cost dental services.

Utilities

NEXT TO GROCERIES, our utility bill was the next largest item in our budget that fluctuated. That meant that I could change it and perhaps save money. With some research and a few simple changes, we were able to reduce our overall utility bill by 25%.

First we had a free energy audit on our home by our local utility company. They reviewed our usage patterns over the past year and made recommendations for energy savings. The most enlightening information was how much energy each appliance was costing. This determined the order that I was going to work on our energy expenses. Below is a chart that shows the energy use of most common household appliances. I based the cost on the kilowatt per hour that it uses and the energy rate for our area. It is meant as a general guideline for your expenses. For a more accurate determination of the costs you are incurring, have your local utility company give your home a free energy audit.

Energy Use Chart

Appliance	Estimated Energy Cost*
Water Heater	
Electric	$50.00–$65.00 per month
Gas	$13.00–$20.00 per month
Refrigerator	
Frost free—16 cubic feet	$19.50 per month
Frost free—20 cubic feet	$23.40 per month
Manual defrost—10 cubic feet	$8.00 per month
Frost free—side by side	$26.00–$39.00 per month

Appliance	Estimated Energy Cost*
Freezer	
Frost free—15 cubic feet	$20.00 per month
Manual defrost—15 cubic feet	$12.00 per month
Washing Machine (full load)	
Cold water only	$0.16 per load
Warm wash, cold rinse	$0.23 per load
Hot wash, warm rinse	$0.36 per load
Clothes Dryer	
Electric	$0.70 per load
Gas	$0.16 per load
Central Heating	
Furnace – small home	$16.00–$40.00 per month
	$0.40 per hour
Furnace – large home	$40.00–$200.00 per month
Electric – small home	$55.00–$110.00 per month
Electric – large home	$110.00–$400.00 per month
Central Cooling	
Window air conditioner	$25.00–$75.00 per month
Central air conditioner	$74.00–$220.00 per month
Electric blanket	$2.10–$4.00 per month
Dishwasher	
gas water heater	$0.23 per load
electric water heater	$0.49 per load
Oven	
gas	$0.06 per hour
electric	$0.16 per hour
Rangetop burner	
gas	$0.04 per hour
electric	$0.15 per hour
Toaster Oven	$0.06 per hour

Appliance	Estimated Energy Cost*
Microwave oven	$0.15 per hour
Electric frying pan	$0.13 per hour
Lighting	
Incandescent bulb, 100 watts	$0.01 per hour
Fluorescent bulb, 27 watts	$0.0025 per hour
Computer	$0.01–$0.02 per hour
Television, color	$0.02–$0.06 per hour
Television, black and white	$0.01 per hour
VCR	$0.01 per hour
Radio	$0.008 per hour
Stereo	$0.02 per hour
Toaster	$0.01 per use
Vacuum cleaner	$0.10 per hour
Iron	$0.13 per hour

*Based on a cost of $0.13 per kwh.
Most of this information came from my local utility company.

COST-SAVING MEASURES

Below are some changes that can be easily implemented in most homes.

Water Heater

Turning down the temperature of your water heater saves more than you think. For every 10° that you turn the heater down, you can save 6–10% of its energy costs. Most energy advisors recommend that you not turn the temperature below 120°. Many automatic dishwashers require a minimum temperature of 120° in order to function properly. Check your dishwashing manual for specific requirements.

Many people wash their dishes by hand in order to save hot water. Depending on how you hand wash your dishes, it may cost you more to wash by hand. If you run the water for each dish to be rinsed, you may be using more hot water than an automatic dishwasher. For maximum savings, fill one basin for washing and one basin for rinsing and turn the water off.

The water heater's location is key to it's best performance. If it is far from the appliances that use it most (like in a garage), much of the energy is wasted as the water travels in the pipes. You can waste 10-15% of the energy used to heat the water by having it travel. If moving the water heater is too costly, insulate the pipes that carry the water to the appliances

For other ways to reduce the costs of your water heater, try these:

- *Wrap the heater in a special insulating blanket.*
- *Install an appliance timer that turns the water heater off during non-use hours (like sleeping hours and vacations).*
- *Reduce the use of hot water where you can—showering accounts for 30% of hot water use in most homes; laundry accounts for 14% of hot water use in most homes.*
- *Don't use the rinse/hold function on your dishwasher. Rinse them yourself, in cold water.*
- *If you need to replace the water heater, make sure the new one has a high energy efficiency rating. Even if other water heaters are cheaper, the higher energy efficiency rating will pay off.*

Water

Since fresh water is only a small percentage of the water available on this planet, we need to use it wisely. Saving money is another good motivator. I have lived through two drought periods and can never go back to wasting water the way I used to. Many of us don't realize how much we are using.

Outdoors, much of our water is lost to evaporation. We put mulch around the plants and trees to trap the moisture in the ground. We timed sprinklers to go on at night so that little was lost to heat. We replaced our kid's sprinkler games with squirt gun games. We wash the car with a nozzle that shuts off between washes. We don't wash the patio if we can sweep it instead.

Indoors, we try to double on baths for the littlest kids. They don't get too dirty and can either share a bath or use the tub one after the other.

We wash clothes only when they need it. Some folks find it easier to throw clothes in the hamper than hanging them up at the end of the day. Fill a plastic jug with water and sink it in the toilet tank. This saves close to the amount of water a low-flush toilet uses.

We like baths but know that showers would save us much water usage. A shower uses four times less water than a bath. And a low-flow shower head can save you another 40% on water usage. A tub with less water will be as thrifty as a shower. My husband's long showers probably cost as much as my kids full tubs.

The dishwasher uses 10–15 gallons of water per washing, so only run it when needed and if full. Don't use the rinse/hold function when you can rinse them yourself before loading.

Here are some more ideas for water savings:

- *When taking a shower, wet yourself, turn the water off, wash, then turn the water on to rinse.*
- *Reduce the number of showers and baths taken by replacing them with sponge baths.*
- *Don't let the water run while brushing teeth or shaving.*
- *Fix any leaking faucets and running toilets. These can lead up to dozens of gallons wasted per day.*
- *Install aerators on all faucets.*
- *Don't use running water to thaw frozen meat. Let them sit in cold water.*
- *Run the washing machine with full loads only.*

Laundry

Most of the expenses of doing laundry come from creating heat— the heat of the water and the heat of the dryer. You can reduce the washing machine's energy usage by 90% by washing and rinsing in cold water only. The average cost of washing and drying a load of laundry is $1 per load. That is based on a cold water wash and an electric dryer.

To maximize the savings with your laundry, try these ideas:

- *Always wash a full load. The cost of washing two medium loads does not equal one full load.*
- *Always dry a full load, but don't overfill the dryer. Air needs to circulate between the clothes.*
- *Line dry whenever you can. Purchase a drying rack for indoor drying in the winter. To soften towels, run them in the dryer for a few minutes, then line dry.*
- *Dry like fabrics together so the dryer will quit sooner. One towel in a load of permanent press clothes will keep the whole load running longer.*
- *Dry loads of clothes one after the other, capturing the heat already in the dryer.*
- *Make sure that the dryer vent is straight. A bent one will reduce air flow and dryer efficiency.*
- *Clean the lint out after every load. Lint reduces air flow and the dryer has to work harder to do the job.*
- *Check with your utility company for discounts on energy during off peak hours. Only run the appliances during those hours to save even more.*

Heating

To efficiently heat a house, you must stop air from leaking in where it isn't welcome. Air leaks are one of the major wastes of energy. They usually cost you another 10% in energy costs. I found them around our doors and windows, and in my fireplace damper. Anywhere two sections meet in a house (a wall and a window, a wall and a door, a vent and a ceiling, etc.) is a good place to check for an air leak. To find if there is a leak, there are several easy ways to tell. The quickest way is to light a candle and slowly move it around the edges of the opening. If it flickers, there is an air leak. Please be careful not to set the curtains on fire as you do this. For a safer way, have someone blow air with a hair dryer around edges while you are outside feeling for the air.

Once I found where my leaks were, I sealed them up with felt weather stripping found at most hardware stores. For some joints I used caulking. This is especially helpful outside for sealing around the joints between the walls and foundation, or the meeting of the brick and walls. For the fireplace, there are foam blocks you can buy to put in the damper door to seal any cracks. Check for fire hazards before using caulk or any permanent materials in the fireplace. The whole weatherizing treatment cost $15. My central heater used to go on four times per night, but now only goes on one time per night, adding up to at least a 10% reduction in our energy bill.

Other ideas for reducing heating costs:

- *Change or clean your heater's filter every month that it is used. Dust gathers and makes the heater work harder to heat the rooms. This will save you 15% of your heating costs.*

- *Plant trees for sun and wind protection. Get a tree that sheds leaves in the winter so that it blocks sun on the house in the summer and lets the sun shine on the house in the winter. This could save you 10–30% in heating and cooling costs.*

- *Insulate your attic and walls to the highest R-value that your county building code recommends. This will reduce your heating costs by 20–30%.*

- *Close the damper on your fireplace after the ashes are cold. This could reduce your heating loss by 10%.*

- *Check if there is a draft or excessive heat (such as a fireplace) near the thermostat in the house. It may be kicking the heater/cooler on when the rest of the house is fine.*

- *Turn the thermostat down and wear more warm clothing. For every degree that you lower the thermostat, you save 3% on energy costs. (Use caution when turning down the heat if you are ill or elderly. It may not be medically advised, or in the case of the elderly, some can easily suffer hypothermia with minor temperature reduction).*

- *Close off the vent and shut doors to rooms not being used.*

- *If you are moving to a new home, consider a bi-level house instead of a long ranch style house. Heat escapes through the roof, so the more roof surface you have, the more heat loss you will have.*

- *Consider an attic fan to suck the hot air out and circulate air in the house. These drop the temperature in a house by at least 10° with little energy usage. In the winter they can keep heating bills lower as well.*

- *Avoid using the fireplace for heating; 90% of the heat that a fire generates goes up the chimney. Fireplaces also tend to suck out the warm air inside the house. Install glass doors over the fireplace that allow heat in but not take house heat out with the fire. Or invest in a stove insert that uses and distributes heat efficiently.*

- *If wood is plentiful and cheap in your area, and you have a fireplace stove, wood would be a cheaper source of heating than electricity or gas.*

The Kitchen

The first thing I did to conserve energy in my kitchen was to get rid of the extra freezer that I had. It wasn't actually in my kitchen (it was in the garage), but I consider it an extension of my kitchen as it held all my extra food. When the energy audit revealed that it was responsible for 15–20% of my utility bill, I questioned its cost effectiveness. I figured it was costing $20 per month to run. I was buying in bulk and storing food in there, but the savings on bulk foods was being spent on the appliance to store them in. This seemed illogical. At that time in our family, we needed every dollar we could save and $20 could help pay off another bill, or pay for 4–5 meals.

I was determined to find a way to do without it. I made more frequent trips to the day-old bread store (or whatever other special bulk purchase), instead of once a month. This way I didn't need to store as much food. I learned to freeze meals in plastic bags and lay them flat so the foods took up less room in the freezer. I purchased a wire rack and created a shelf in the small freezer section of my refrigerator. This gave me more storage space. Once I was confident that I could do it, I sold the freezer.

When I cook, I can easily conserve energy with some minor changes. When I bake, I try to bake several things at once, so that the oven is not on just for one dish. For smaller dishes, the microwave or toaster oven are more energy efficient. I don't preheat the oven unless I am baking breads. I try not to peek at the food while cooking, since I lose as much as 20% of the heat trapped in there. If you have a self-cleaning oven, clean it right after you are done baking. You are using the heat already trapped in the oven. For maximum air circulation, make sure the racks in the oven are not covered in foil. Any blockage of the air movement means the oven will heat unevenly and give false temperature readings.

For range top cooking, the pan should match the burner size. A small pan on a large burner will waste 40% of the heat generated. By using a lid on all pans, you can use three times less energy to cook that dish. Copper-bottomed pans heat up faster and require less energy to cook foods.

Other ideas for saving energy in the kitchen:

- *If you have a choice between gas or electric ranges and ovens, the gas version will save you money. Do not consider remodeling just for that reason without having a professional compare the savings you will gain over the cost of the remodeling.*
- *A gas range/oven with an automatic ignition saves 40–50% more than a pilot light.*
- *Turn off the range or oven before the food is done cooking. Heat still remains on the burner.*
- *Boil water on the range, not in the microwave oven. It uses more energy to do the job and they take about the same amount of time.*
- *Broiling is more energy efficient than baking.*
- *Check with your utility company for discounts on energy during off peak hours. Only run the oven during those hours to save even more.*
- *Bake and run the dishwasher in the evening in summer to avoid heating up the house. In the winter, do these activities in the morning (to help heat up the house).*

Lighting

Most light bulbs are incandescent. These are inefficient makers of light. They use 10% of their energy for producing light, and 90% are wasted on heat that they produce. Fluorescent bulbs use 65–75% less energy to produce light, and they last 10 times longer than an incandescent bulb. The Energy Use Chart earlier in the chapter can be deceptive when we talk about lighting costs. It says that we only spend one cent per hour on light bulbs that are turned on. We tend to forget how quickly this adds up. We usually have several bulbs on and we tend to leave them on for several hours. This can add up to as much as 30% of your utility bill.

If converting your lighting fixtures to fluorescent isn't in your budget, try some of the fluorescent bulbs made to screw in lamp sockets. These can save wherever they fit. If you are stuck with incandescent bulb usage, try these ideas to reduce some of the costs:

- *Clear light bulbs give off more light than frosted versions.*
- *Many bulbs can be replaced by a lower watt bulb, and still meet your lighting needs.*
- *When buying bulbs, don't go by the wattage. The lumens determine how much light is produced. Each bulb has a lumen number on it as well.*
- *A light lampshade will allow more light into the room.*
- *If you are working in a room, just light that area with a work lamp or reading lamp above you. The whole room doesn't need to be lit.*
- *Turn off lights when you leave a room.*
- *Avoid the long-life bulbs. They cost you more in the long run because they use more energy. Stick with less expensive lower watt bulbs.*
- *If you have fluorescent lights, don't turn them on and off frequently. That shortens the life of the bulb. Leave them on if you will return to the room soon.*

Special Needs

T HERE ARE MANY FOLKS with special needs in their diet, as a result of allergies or a chemical reaction to the additives in the foods.

Many people (children in particular) react to some of the more than 5000 additives in our foods. It's not surprising since these additives are chemicals and not natural elements found in nature. Most additives are petroleum derivatives. Other people have allergies to items commonly found in most of the prepared foods (such as corn). In order to work around these elements, people must find alternatives to items normally bought and taken for granted. For example, instead of buying the crackers (or whatever) that are on sale that week, only specific name brands can be eaten that are known not to have additives. This can raise the price of your grocery bill.

We experienced this challenge a few years ago. Our son reacts to any additives in food, or the air (perfume, solvents, fumes, etc.). We needed to buy only foods that were additive-free. This did not mean I could only shop at health food stores. I found most of our needs at local stores. But it did mean that I could no longer pick up the generic brand or the weekly special. This put a big crimp in our penny-pinching ways. This new challenge required an even deeper adherence to the 11 guidelines for a miserly way of life.

I have had several people express doubt that they can eat healthy and only spend half of what they usually spend for groceries. It can be done. It takes even more planning and shopping around than the average miserly mom. You can't just drop into a health food store with your shopping list and expect to save any money. Our newest challenge in shopping helped prove to others that it can be done.

To keep within my grocery budget, I needed to plan even more carefully. I can never fall back on a convenience food or restaurant meal because of the additives. This alone is an incentive to stay true to my guidelines. I can never say, "I'm too tired to cook from scratch, or too tired to shop." Any brand of food is not an option. I have to watch all the local flyers for sales on the foods we can eat. I have to shop at several stores to buy the certain brands or types of foods in our dietary guidelines on sale. I use co-ops for the items only available at costly health food stores.

I make more of our own foods now, than when I first started with the 11 guidelines. We eat less meat and poultry, replacing them with dried bean, whole grain, or stir-fry meals. This reduces our overall costs. We stretch leftovers into another meal. I try to cook several meals at once and freeze them.

So when I hear people complain that it's too much work to save money, I think back to when we didn't know about this additive problem. Reaching that goal was so much easier than it is now. But anyone can do it. There is help for this type of challenging cooking and shopping; agencies and support groups have researched the additive topic. If you help, or want more information on the reactions commonly experienced by food additives, contact the Feingold Association: West Coast (415) 572-7575 or East Coast (703) 768-3287. They specialize in the reactions (medical, emotional and physical) that people have to additives. They have cookbooks and shopping lists to help make shopping easier to live with.

Whatever your special dietary need, the eleven guidelines can help keep you within your budget. You might have to work harder than most, or be a little more creative, but they will prove helpful for any situation.

Crafts For Kids

T HERE ARE MANY DAYS that my kids needed something to do. I could buy a craft or some other item, but I found my budget couldn't handle those solutions. It's amazing what a little imagination can do. When I lived in Nigeria and Pakistan, I saw kids make toys out of things they found. So, I researched some ways to make our crafts. My kids appreciate the time I have invested: The cost is minimal, and we have fun together. Below are some ideas that we have enjoyed.

KIDS' APRONS

I don't believe in buying a special apron for kids (unless it's at a garage sale or given to me). They are expensive and the kids grow out of them quickly. Instead of a ready made apron, we use something we already have. When my husband is through with one of his long sleeved shirts, we turn it into a paint or craft apron. The kids wear it backwards (so the buttons are in the back) and we slightly roll up the cuffs. The shirt is long enough to cover their clothes well, and we have saved $8–$15.

BUBBLES THAT LAST

> 1/2 CUP LIQUID DAWN OR JOY
> 2 T. GLYCERIN (AT DRUG STORES)
> 5 CUPS WATER

Pour water into container first. Add dish soap and glycerin and stir (try not to make it froth). Dip bubble wand in and blow!

BUBBLE WANDS: For homemade bubble wands try bending wire in any shape (a coat hanger works).

BIRD COOKIES

WOODEN TREE ORNAMENTS OR SHAPES (1/4 INCH THIN)
PEANUT BUTTER
BIRD SEEDS

Poke a hole in the top of the shape to string. Lather wooden shapes with peanut butter. Roll in bird seed. Hang outside where you can watch the birds eat.

BIRD TREATS

1/2 CUP PEANUT BUTTER
1/2 CUP FLOUR
1-1/2 CUP BIRDSEED

Mix well and shape into ball. Press to 1/2 inch thick. Place on baking sheet. Gently poke a hole in the middle of the "cookie." Bake at 425° for 30 minutes. Cool completely. Hang with string outside.

HOW TO MAKE PAPER

This is not only a craft, but a lesson in science (recycling, that is).

What you need:

SEVERAL PIECES OF PAPER (NEWSPAPER, BINDER PAPER, OR EVEN PAPER BAGS)
SOME WINDOW SCREEN ON A FRAME (SCREEN CAN BE BOUGHT AT THE HARDWARE STORE AND ART STORES SELL PLAIN WOODEN FRAMES—THEN USE A STAPLE GUN TO ATTACH THE SCREENING MATERIAL TO THE WOODEN FRAME.)
A BUCKET OR DEEP PAN
A BLENDER
A MAGNIFYING GLASS
DRY NEWSPAPER OR FELT

What to do:

Tear up the paper into bits. Soak paper for several hours in water. Fill a blender with the paper and water mixture from the bucket. Blend the paper until you see pulp. You can see the wood fibers if you look at the pulp under the magnifying glass.

Hold your screen over a wide container or sink and pour pulp onto the screen. Spread pulp around evenly. Lay some felt or newspaper on top of the pulp and gently press all around the pulp, soaking up the water. Turn the screen over, holding the newspaper on the bottom. Lay on a tabletop covered with more newspaper or a towel. Put newspaper over the top and repeat the pressing procedure. Repeat all of these steps until the pulp is fairly dry. Lift off the newspaper and the screen carefully. Allow to dry overnight.

Fun things to try:

- *Add 1 tablespoon of laundry starch to make the paper smoother.*
- *Add decorations to the paper pulp before pouring on the screen.*

LEAF PAINTING

Collect leaves of different types and vein patterns. Paint an even coat of non-toxic paint on top of a sponge. Place the ribbed side of the leaf on top of the sponge. Place a piece of paper on the leaf and press gently for 10–15 seconds. Place the leaf, paint side down, on a piece of paper. Place another piece of paper on top and rub gently for another 10–15 seconds. Remove top paper carefully, and carefully peel off leaf, holding by its stem.

TORN PAPER ART

Save single sheets of colored paper or construction paper that isn't being used. I save fliers that arrive on colored paper that have no print on one side. Tear them into small pieces (1/4 inch each). Draw a basic outline on a sheet of white paper of what you want to make (such as a Christmas tree, a wreath, a boat, etc.), and glue the torn pieces of paper into the design.

We made a Christmas tree by drawing a triangle for the tree and filling it in with torn green pieces, then adding a few red and blue pieces for ornaments, and a few brown pieces (from a brown paper bag) for the trunk.

MODELING DOUGH

Kids can help mix this. Add more fun by using rolling pins, and cookie cutters.

Ingredients:

> 1–1/2 CUPS FLOUR
> 1/2 CUP SALT
> FOOD COLORING (OPTIONAL)
> 1/2 CUP WATER
> 1/4 CUP VEGETABLE OIL

Mix the flour and salt in a mixing bowl. In a separate bowl, put your water and a few drops of food coloring. Stir the coloring to mix. Add oil to the water, then combine with the flour mixture. Mix well and knead the dough until soft.

Tips:

- *Sprinkle with a little flour and knead in if dough is too sticky.*
- *Leftover dough can be stored in plastic bags or airtight containers to keep it soft.*

PLAY DOUGH

(This is like the above recipe, but has a slightly different texture, and lasts longer).

Ingredients:

> 2 CUPS FLOUR
> 1 CUP SALT
> 4 TSP. CREAM OF TARTAR
> 2 CUPS WATER WITH FOOD COLORING
> 2 T. OIL

Mix together in a pan (non-stick is better). Cook over medium heat until it forms a hard ball. Knead when warm for a smoother consistency.

As it becomes half-cooked, the dough is hard to mix. Keep stirring until all parts are hardened. This batch of play dough will cost only 25¢ as compared to between $1.00–$2.50 for store bought.

Tip:

- *Add glitter for glitter dough. Add when cooking is finished and you are kneading dough.*
- *Use unsweetened drink mix for the coloring. It also adds fragrance. Use 1–2 packs for each recipe.*

PEANUT BUTTER MODELING CLAY

1 CUP PEANUT BUTTER
1 CUP NONFAT DRY MILK
2/3 CUP POWDERED SUGAR

Measure the peanut butter and dry milk in a large bowl and mix well. Add powdered sugar and work in with fingers. If it's too dry, add peanut butter. If it's too sticky, add dry milk. Try making spiders by rolling a ball for the tummy and one for the head. Use pretzel sticks for the legs and raisins for the eyes. Or make snakes by rolling it between your hands.

SALT-FLOUR DOUGH

2 CUPS SALT
3 CUPS FLOUR
1 1/2 CUPS WATER (APPROXIMATE)
BAKING SHEET

Mix the salt and flour in a bowl. Add water until the dough is moldable. You don't want it too wet, or it will take a long time to dry.

Spread the mixture on the baking sheet in any pattern desired. After the dough dries (1-3 days), paint with acrylic paints.

AROMATIC MODELING DOUGH

This is fun to make at Christmas time. One woman makes it into a pie crust, with the top layer latticed, and potpourri inside the "pie."

> 3/4 CUP APPLESAUCE
> 1 CUP CINNAMON (4 OZ.)
> 1 T. CLOVES
> 1 T. NUTMEG
> 2 T. GLUE

Mix thoroughly, and shape into figures (snowmen, bowls, etc.). Lay on cookie sheet and leave in oven, with only oven light on, over night (or turn on 150° for a few hours).

PAINT WITH PEBBLES

Collect smooth stones. Paint with acrylic. Glue eyes on to make faces. Cover with clear nail polish after the paint is dry.

Make a family by hot gluing several people to a piece of driftwood.

ROCK CANDY

This is fun, and teaches patience, too.

Ingredients:

> A HEAT-RESISTANT JAR
> 1 CUP WATER
> 3 3-1/2 CUPS SUGAR
> 3 CLEAN STRINGS, 10 INCHES EACH
> A PENCIL

Boil water in a pan. Add the sugar. Stir until a syrup forms. Be careful that the syrup doesn't boil over. When the sugar is dissolved, remove the heat and cool for 10 minutes. Pour into glass jar.

Tie one end of each string to the pencil, leaving a space between strings. Rest the pencil over the jar, dropping the strings into the syrup.

Check the jar every day, but don't move the strings. Crystals will form in about 2 weeks. If crystals cover the surface of the water, break them up carefully, so further evaporation will continue.

FIREWORKS IN JANUARY

Color a piece of paper with red, blue, and green crayons (color in large patches of each color). Cover all of the paper. Paint over it with black poster paint or ink. Let it dry. Scratch off firework shapes with a toothpick.

STREET CHALK

> *1 CUP PLASTER OF PARIS (DO NOT PACK)*
> *ALMOST 1/2 CUP COOL WATER*
> *2–3 T. LIQUID ACRYLIC PAINT*
> *DIXIE CUPS*

Pour plaster into a disposable container. Using a disposable stirring stick, stir in most of the water. Add paint and mix well. Add a little more water as the mixture thickens. Stir well and pour into Dixie cups. Peel off the paper when the chalk is dry.

JUICE LIDS

Ever wonder what to do with those concentrated juice can lids (the little round metal discs)? Here are a few ideas:

- *Make refrigerator magnets by decorating the front with the following ideas. Small magnets can be purchased by the pack at most craft stores.*
  - *paint with different colored fabric glue*
  - *paint on a thin layer of white glue, and cover with sand. Shake off excess. When dry, paste a cut-out camel or other desert animal*
  - *take a favorite wallet sized photo and cut into the shape of the lid. Glue it to the lid.*

- *Create sorting toys for younger kids. Save any container that has a lid (oatmeal box, yogurt container, etc.) and cut a slit in the lid. Let the little ones put them in the box one at a time.*

GOOP

This is much like Gak® found in toy stores, but this recipe will not stain everything that it touches, and it easily washes out of fabrics. It also makes a great science project, since it is a chemical reaction. The home-made version costs about $1.25 versus the storebought version at $4–$6.

> 8 OZ. ELMERS GLUE (USE SCHOOL GLUE, NOT GLUE ALL OR WASHABLE GLUE)
> 3/4 CUP WATER PLUS FOOD COLORING
> 1 TSP. 20 MULE TEAM BORAX (IN MOST LAUNDRY AISLES OF GROCERY STORE)
> 1/2 CUP WATER

In a large bowl, combine the first 3 ingredients until well blended. In a separate cup, combine the borax and water until the borax is dissolved. Pour the borax solution into the glue and stir. A large lump will form. Work the lump with your hands, occasionally rubbing into the remaining glue. As you work the lump, the glue will be absorbed, and the lump will become smooth. Store in an airtight plastic box or zippered plastic bag. It will last a few weeks.

Cleaning Tip:

If the Goop gets on clothing or fabric, wash before it dries. Spraying with a pretreatment helps. If the Goop dries and hardens before you notice, soak the area overnight, scraping off as much as possible, and spraying with a pretreatment. This may require a few washes.

CREEPY SLIME

> 1 CUP CORNSTARCH
> 1/2 CUP COLD WATER
> FOOD COLORING

Mix in bowl. Put in your hand and it slowly creeps. Pound on it on the table and it's solid. Which is it?

SILLY PUTTY

> *1/4 CUP LIQUID LAUNDRY STARCH*
> *1/4 CUP ELMER'S SCHOOL GLUE*

Mix together. This makes enough for a few kids to each have a glob. Some have found that mixing inside a plastic bag works best. Store in a plastic container or in the refrigerator.

FINGER PAINT

> *2 T. CORNSTARCH*
> *2 T. COOL WATER*
> *1 CUP BOILING WATER*
> *FOOD COLORING*

Mix the cool water and cornstarch. Add the boiling water and stir. It should thicken as you stir. When it is cool, divide into small cups, or muffin tins. Then add food coloring and mix.

(To remove any stains these create, try the stain removal ideas in the chapter Safer and Cheaper.)

QUICK AND CHEAP FINGER PAINT

Mix a few drops of food coloring with some shaving cream. The kids can color on paper, or in the bathtub on the tile. This is an easier place to clean up.

MOO-VING MILK

> *1/2 CUP WHOLE MILK*
> *FEW DROPS FOOD COLORING*
> *FEW DROPS LIQUID DETERGENT*

Pour milk in a pie plate or bowl. Drop some food coloring in the milk, but don't let the drops touch each other. Add a few drops of detergent, and watch the colors swirl. Why is this happening? The detergent is causing the milk fat to separate.

Safer and Cheaper

S TORE SHELVES ARE FILLED with products we are told we "need" to use in order to effectively clean our homes. Most of them do a great job. But at what price? What's more important to know, is that they aren't necessary in order to do a good job of cleaning.

THE TRUE COST OF STORE BOUGHT CLEANERS

The first cost is to the people.

The chemicals in these cleaners are diluted forms of caustic and dangerous elements. The effect on us is not entirely known at this time.

The second cost is financial.

Most cleaners can be replaced with common household items. These common ingredients cost pennies compared to the dollars these cleaners cost.

The third cost is to the environment.

We flush these chemicals down the drain and into the water supply. Many municipal water treatment plants don't filter these out.

I began to research alternative cleaners, not out of interest in the environment, but to combat my son's chemical sensitivity. The more I use them, the happier I am at the effect on the environment, my kids, and my pocket book. There are many good books in the library filled with recipes for cleaners. Below are some of the best recipes I have found.

We don't need special cleaning products for each cleaning need. We don't need a special bottle for tile cleaning, and one for the toilet, and another for counter tops, floors or walls, etc. The cleaning supply manufacturers want you to think you need these so they make more money. Many of these share the same ingredients.

ALTERNATIVE CLEANERS

With some basic supplies you can do most of your cleaning. Here is a list of the basic supplies that I use, and a description of their purpose:

Vinegar

This inexpensive ingredient kills bacteria and mold and can be used as a disinfectant, but without the risk. Use distilled for a less offensive odor. Soak cloth diapers in it, instead of ammonia. This also can be used to remove soap scum, or wash windows, and added to dishwater to make glass sparkle. It can be used as a stain remover. It has many first aid uses such as bee stings, hives, sunburn, gargle for sore throats, and upset stomachs. The chemical name for vinegar is acetic acid.

Baking Soda

This is a versatile, non-toxic cleaner. It can be a non-scratch powder for scrubbing metal and tile surfaces. Diluted in water, it deodorizes and cleans refrigerators, thermoses, etc. Sprinkle on carpets to remove odors. It can put out a grease fire by sprinkling on the flame. There are literally hundreds of uses for baking soda. If you are interested, look up "baking soda" at your local library for books on its uses.

Borax/Washing Soda

This is a natural compound that does many things. It is a cleaner and a water softener. It can be used to scrub metal and tile surfaces without scratching. It can be poured in drains to keep them clean. It kills fleas. It cleans floors well. It is great for neutralizing the ammonia in urine when soaking diapers.

Citrus Peels

Citrus is a fragrant cleaning source. The fruit can be ground up in garbage disposals to freshen and clear out the gunk built up in there. The peels can be boiled and the solution used for cleaning greasy messes, not to mention freshening the air. A manufacturer has bottled this idea in an all natural solvent called Citra-Solv®.

CLEANING RECIPES

Below are my favorite cleaning recipes that are simple to make.

Furniture Polish

1 PART LEMON JUICE
2 PARTS VEGETABLE OR OLIVE OIL

Brass Polish

Apply ketchup or Worcestershire sauce. Let stand a few minutes, then rinse. If an area doesn't clean, there must be a build up of grease or dirt. Clean the residue off with a paste of salt and vinegar, then reapply the sauce. Or try a natural product called Citra-Solv®, made from citrus peels.

Copper Polish

Mix equal parts warm vinegar with salt. Scrub away then rinse. Good for brass as well.

Silver Polish

Make a paste with 1/4 cup baking soda and 1–1/2 T. water. Apply with a damp sponge. Rub, then rinse and buff dry.

Put the baking soda in enough boiling water to cover the silverware. Let sit 10 minutes, then polish.

Drain Cleaner

1/4 CUP BAKING SODA
1/2 CUP VINEGAR

Pour baking soda in drain. Pour vinegar in drain. Tightly close the drain. Let rest a few minutes. Then flush with boiling water. Repeat until clear.

To keep the drain free of build up, weekly flush with 1/4 cup salt, then boiling water.

Hard Water Build up

Put equal parts vinegar and water inside a tea kettle or vase that has mineral build up in it. Let sit for at least 1/2 hour. Then scrub out the minerals.

Oven Cleaner

When the spill still is warm, sprinkle with salt and scrub.

Tile and Floor Cleaner

Scrub with a paste of Borax and water.

Carpet Cleaner

> 1 PART CORNMEAL
> 1 PART BORAX MULE TEAM

Combine and sprinkle over carpet. Leave on for one hour. Vacuum.

Nilodor/Nilogel

There is a product that absorbs soaked in spills. It is made of gel crystals that you shake over the spill. They absorb the liquid in a few minutes and then you sweep or vacuum it up. Call (800) 443-4321 for more information.

Carpet Odor

Sprinkle baking soda on the carpet and leave overnight. Vacuum well.

Upholstery Cleaner

> 1/4 CUP BORAX
> 1 T. DISH WASHING LIQUID
> 1 CUP WARM WATER

Rub with a soft cloth that has been dipped in this solution.

Wall Cleaner

> 1 GALLON HOT WATER
> 1/2 CUP BORAX

My Great Grandma Maggie's Porcelain Cleaner

Rub porcelain with cream of tartar and damp, soft rag.

Window Cleaner #1

2 CUPS WATER
2 T. AMMONIA

Window Cleaner #2

1 CUP VINEGAR
2 CUPS WATER

Both of these recipes clean windows and mirrors great!

Toilet Bowl

Sprinkle with baking soda, then pour on a little vinegar. Scrub with a brush. For tougher stains, make a paste of Borax and lemon juice and let sit on the stain overnight.

General Spot Remover

This solution is good for blood, chocolate, coffee, mildew, and mud. Dissolve 1/4 cup Borax in 2 cups cold water. Sponge on and let dry. Wash as recommended.

Ink

Wet with water, then apply a paste of cream of tartar and lemon juice. Let sit for an hour, then wash. Also try spraying with hair spray right before washing.

"Washable" Color Markers

Rinse stain in cold water until it runs clear. Then wet the stain with rubbing alcohol. Blot the stain with another cloth until the color is removed. Wash in hottest water as allowed for the fabric.

Poster Paints and Watercolors on Garments

Apply rubbing alcohol to the stain and blot with another cloth until no more comes off. Allow to line dry.

If the stain remains, soak garment in 1 quart warm water, 1 tsp. of dish washing liquid and 1 T. of vinegar. Wash in as hot a water temperature as the fabric can tolerate.

Poster Paint, Finger Paint and Watercolors on Carpeting or Clothing

First remove as much of the paint as possible by making a paste of baking soda and water. Cover the stain. When the paste is dry, vacuum the spot. To remove what remains, soak a sponge in rubbing alcohol and blot the stain until no more comes on the sponge (I stand on my sponge to encourage the paint to soak up). If there is still some stain left, blot again with a sponge soaked in ammonia.

Silly Putty in Carpeting or Garments

My mom says that when I left Silly Putty in the carpet, she froze it by applying ice. It became brittle and peeled right off.

Chewing Gum in Hair

Lather peanut butter on the gum. It will dissolve the gum. Comb out. Keep doing this until all is out. Also try freezing it like with the Silly Putty above.

Play Dough in Carpeting

Remove larger pieces while dough is still pliable. Let the rest dry overnight into the carpet. Make a solution of warm water with some dish washing soap. Use a stiff brush dipped in the water to work the rest of the dough out.

Lipstick

Rub with shortening (not margarine—this has yellow dye in it) and clean with washing soda.

Bath Time

For a soothing bath, put one cup dry milk in the tub.

Toothpaste

For a simple and quick paste:

Mix equal parts baking soda and salt. For flavor, add a dash of cinnamon, mint extract or flavored fluoride liquid.

Or try this mixture:

    8 T. BAKING SODA
    3 T. GLYCERIN (AVAILABLE AT DRUG STORES)
    1-2 TSP. FLAVORING (PEPPERMINT, ORANGE, ETC.)

Blend well and store in airtight container.

Liquid Soap
as given to me by Deborah Tukua, editor of *Coming Home* magazine

> *1 BAR SOAP (4-6 OZ.)*
> *1 T. HONEY*
> *1 TSP. GLYCERIN*
> *WATER*

Directions:
1. Grate one bar of soap in the blender. Soap should appear as small flakes.
2. add 1 c. boiling water and whip in blender.
3. Add 1/2 c. of tap water (unheated) and stir in blender.
4. Add 1 T. honey and 1 tsp. glycerin and stir in blender.
5. Let cool (approximately 15 min.), then whip again. Mixture should be approximately 2 cups. Add cooled water to blender until mixture reaches the 5-6 cup mark and whip.
6. Pour mixture into container(s) for storage and allow to cool without the lids on for at least an hour. Mixture will thicken as it sets up. Shake before using.

Note: Herbs can be steeped in boiling water before adding to the grated soap if desired (such as chamomile or lavender or fresh pine needles which will need to be strained out after the steeping process).

Cleansing Cream
> *3 T. COCONUT OIL*
> *1 T. VEGETABLE OIL*
> *2 TSP. WATER*

Melt these on low heat. Remove from heat and beat with a whisk or fork until well blended. Store in airtight jar. If your house becomes very hot, keep in the refrigerator. Coconut oil melts at low temperatures.

Astringent
I have heard three ways to make astringent. Below are all three for you to choose from. My favorite is the first. It is very refreshing.

> *MIX EQUAL PARTS WITCH HAZEL AND WATER*
> *OR*
> *MIX EQUAL PARTS DISTILLED WHITE VINEGAR AND WATER*
> *OR*
> *MASH SOME STRAWBERRIES AND RUB ON YOUR FACE. RINSE WITH WARM WATER.*

Bee Stings/Sunburn/Hives

Vinegar can instantly relieve the pain and itch of bee stings, hives, or sunburn much faster than a baking soda paste. Soak the paper from a brown paper bag with vinegar and lay on the affected area.

Antacid

> 1/2 TSP. BAKING SODA
> 1/2 CUP WATER

For an upset stomach, combine and drink.

Allergies

If airborne particles irritate your nose, try this remedy. Take a Q-Tip and dab a thin layer of petroleum jelly on the inside of each nostril, at least one inch inside. It grabs some of the offensive pollens.

Cuts and Burns

Use good cleanliness on an injury and you should fare well. Avoid the remedies such as iodine, hydrogen peroxide, merthiolate, mercurochrome, Bactine, Campho-Phenique. These damage the skin and can lead to worse scaring.

Ice Bag

> 2 QUART SIZE ZIPPERED PLASTIC BAG
> 1 CUP WATER
> 1/2 CUB RUBBING ALCOHOL

Put liquid in one bag and seal tightly. Put the other bag around it and seal it for double protection. Freeze. It will be slushy so it can mold to the wounded area. Leave on the skin for 10–20 minutes. Be careful of causing frost bite on the skin.

My Great Grandma Maggie's Remedy for Arthritis Pain

Mix rubbing alcohol with a few drops of wintergreen and rub on the parts affected.

Athlete's Foot

> 1/2 CUP APPLE CIDER VINEGAR
> 2 CUPS HOT WATER

Soak your feet in the solution until it cools. Do this once a day for about a week, or until the fungi are killed.

Skin Irritations

For relief of minor burns, itches from insect bites, sunburn, and poison oak or ivy, rub the area with fresh aloe vera. Keep a plant in the house and break off a branch, releasing the juices inside. Rub directly on the effected area as often as needed.

Yeast Infections

When eaten, the live yogurt culture, acidophilus, is helpful in combating yeast infections.

My Great Grandma Maggie's Remedy for No-Run Stockings

Soak stockings in a mixture of alum and water to prevent running.

Cleaning tools

Instead of spending money for scrubbing tools, see what you can reuse around the house. For example, when a toothbrush begins to fray and would normally be discarded, I put it with my cleaning supplies. I use it for cleaning grout and tight spots around faucets. It also cleans jewelry with gem stones very well.

Grease

To cut grease, tar, or lipstick from most surfaces, try a product called Citra-Solv®. It's totally natural and smells great. It's a concentrated liquid of citrus peels. You can use on engines, stoves, clothes, rugs, etc.

Garden Pesticide

1 T. DISH WASHING DETERGENT
1 CUP VEGETABLE OIL

Mix and store in an airtight container. When needed, mix 1–2 T. solution with 1 cup water.
Spray on plants, covering all leaf and stem surfaces. (From the U.S. Dept. of Agriculture).

Another Garden Pesticide

3 ONIONS
2 QUARTS OF WATER
4 CLOVES OF GARLIC

Boil these together for an hour. When cool, place in a spray bottle and spray on plants.

Snail Bait

2 TSP. SUGAR
1/2 TSP. YEAST
2 CUP WATER

Mix this in a shallow dish, such as a pie pan. Snails are attracted to this bait, and will drown in it.

Weeds

To kill unwanted growths in your garden, pour boiling water directly on the weeds. To save plants around weeds, water good plants and surrounding soil well right before applying the hot water. This cools the plants and if any hot water seeps on to the good plants, the water already in the soil will cool it down. Make sure you pour the hot water only on the weed.

Ants

When these critters visit your house, try the following:

- *first find their attraction, and discard outside*
- *follow the trail to its source*
- *plug the hole with a gel (toothpaste, shaving gel)*
- *wipe the trail clean with a sponge and warm water*
- *sprinkle cornstarch, cinnamon powder, or iodized salt where they are coming in. It works for us!*

Fleas

Fleas can feel like a curse. Especially if you are unable to use the chemical solutions available for this problem. Here are some tested remedies.

For fleas and eggs in the carpets:

- *sprinkle Borax all over the carpet, especially around the edges. Work it into the carpet. Let it sit for 3 days, then vacuum.*
- *sprinkle boric acid all around the edges of the wall. Fleas like*

tight places and lay eggs there. You can buy this in bulk at a hardware store (or drug store sometimes); or you can pay more and buy it at a pet store under the name of The Terminator.

- sprinkle diatomaceous earth (DE) around the carpet and crevices where the wall and floor meet. This cuts their skin and dehydrates them. Don't buy the pool supply type of DE which is dangerous if inhaled.

- steam clean the carpet, then vacuum daily for a few days. The hot water kills most of the eggs and fleas. The others will hatch a few days later from the heat.

- after vacuuming, take the bag out and seal it in a plastic bag. Set in the sun to bake the trapped fleas. I even microwaved mine for 10 seconds.

- lay eucalyptus branches and leaves around the edges of the carpets in the house. It's a natural repellent, and they'll leave in a few days. Bay leaves are suppose to be effective as well.

For fleas on the pet:

- use a flea comb and have a bowl of soapy water or rubbing alcohol to dip the fleas in.

- simmer lemons for 45 minutes, then cool and strain the solution. Wet the pet thoroughly.

Termites

Termites need professional care, but you can take some steps to avoid them.

- don't stack firewood any closer than 10 feet to any part of the house.

- don't use decorative wood chips any closer than 3 feet to the house.

Cockroaches

These are nasty to have around, because they don't go away. These things can help:

- *lay non-poisonous traps called "roach hotels." These have a scent that attracts, and sticky stuff that grabs them and won't let go.*
- *lay sliced cucumber around the cupboards. There is something in the little green vegetable that repels them.*
- *lay bay leaves around the cupboards.*
- *Sprinkle a fine layer of boric acid wherever they might walk. When they clean their feet, they will ingest the element and die within two weeks.*

Menu Plans

T HE FOLLOWING APPENDIX shows it is possible to feed a family of four on $40 per week. The Menu Plan #1 is a single week's menu with an accompanying shopping list. Recipes for the dinners are included in chapter 13, "Some Great Recipes." Menu Plan #2 is a month's meal planning. The meals are listed for your own mix and match choices. The shopping lists are made for each of the stores that I visited that month to make the meals. The prices are what I paid.

MENU PLAN #1

One Week for $40

Day 1	Day 2	Day 3	Day 4	Day 5	Day 6	Day 7
BREAKFAST						
pancake	muffins	muffins	french toast	eggs	cereal	cereal
fruit	fruit	fruit	fruit	fruit	fruit	fruit
milk	milk	milk	milk	milk	milk	milk
LUNCH						
lunch meat	cheese	PBJ	lunch meat	spaghetti*	chicken	soup*
sandwich	& crackers	sandwich	sandwich		salad*	bread
1 fruit	1 fruit	1 fruit	1 fruit	1 fruit	1 fruit	1 fruit

Drinks: pack thermos of homemade lemonade, milk or fruit juice if available
Snack: homemade cookies, crackers, popcorn, carrot sticks, homemade granola bars

DINNER						
Spaghetti	Chicken	Mushroom Chicken	Beans	Chicken	Soup	Leftovers
zucchini	Salad	Mash potatoes	Rice	Pot	Rolls**	smorgasbord
sauce	w/honey	Salad	Salad	Pie	Salad	Salad
French	mustard		Dressing			
Bread	dressing**					
	Rolls**					

*(leftover)   **(homemade)

MENU #1—ONE WEEK FOR $40

Sample Grocery List

2 gl. milk	3.99	2 gallon pack
3 lb. apples	1.80	
10 lb. oranges	1.50	sale
2 lb. banana	.90	
1 dz. eggs	.99	good sale
cheese 1/2 lb	.80	sale/stock up
1 loaf (store brand) bread	.79	
1 loaf french bread	1.29	store brand
1 can frozen lemonade	.79	
box of saltine crackers (1 lb.)	.99	sale/stock up
1 jar salsa	1.59	
2 cups rice (bulk or generic)	.50	
2 cans black beans	1.05	
6 lb. boneless chicken thighs	9.48	warehouse club
4 large potatoes	.50	
1 can cream of mushroom soup	.79	
spaghetti	.50	sale/stock up
spaghetti sauce	.99	sale/stock up
zucchini (6)	1.30	
carrots (1 lb.)	.25	farmer's market/sale
2 onion	.25	
1 lb. flour	.79	sale/stock up
1 can chicken broth	.50	
1 box cereal	1.99	sale/stock up
3 heads of lettuce	1.50	
turkey or lowfat ham lunch meat	2.00	sale
1 32 oz. can pinto beans	1.19	
1 bunch green onions	.20	
1 cup roasted peanuts	.75	
Total	$39.96	

MENU PLAN #2

SAMPLE MENU FOR ONE MONTH
Average Weekly Cost of $40

Key: The numbers in parentheses ( ) show how many times that meal will be served that month.

BREAKFAST

homemade granola (10–12)
homemade cinnamon rolls (2)
muffins
cold boxed cereal (10–12)
hot cereal
french toast
pancakes or waffles

LUNCHES

peanut butter and jelly sandwiches (8)
lunch meat sandwiches (8)
hot dogs (4)
tuna sandwich (2)
cheese and cracker (2)
macaroni and cheese (4)
soup and crackers (3)
homemade tofu nuggets
homemade fries and burgers
bagel & cream cheese (5)

SNACKS & FRUIT

homemade cookies and granola bars
popcorn (caramel, spiced, plain)
rice pudding

VEGETABLES
salad (10)
frozen (10)
fresh (10)

DRINKS:
juices, milk or water

DINNERS
Chinese Noodles
Spaghetti with Meatballs
Pork Roast
Pot Pie (2)
Stir-fry
Leek & Potato Soup (2)
Anne's Squash Casserole
Black Bean Soup (2)
Huevos Rancheros
Leftover Chicken Italian meal (2)
Leftovers Smorgasbord (4)
Vegetarian Chili and homemade cornbread (2)
Easy Microwave Lasagna
Messy Chicken (2)
Indian Curry
Chinese Pineapple Chicken
Pizza (3)
Poor Man Steak

ONE MONTH SHOPPING LIST FOR MENU #2

Averages $40 each week

Grocery Store #1	unit cost	
Loss leaders only		
rice, 2 lb. bag	1x	$1.00
saltine crackers	2x	$0.99
oats (42 oz.)	2x	$1.99
wheat bread	8x	$0.99
apples, 10 lb. bag	1x	$3.50
oranges, 10 lb. bag	1x	$1.50
Total		$19.88

Grocery Store #2	unit cost	
Store coupon book only		
eggs	2x	$0.99
peanut butter	2x	$1.50
black beans, can	4x	$0.49
frozen vegetables		
(5 mixed, 1 pea)	6x	$0.50
flour	2x	$0.99
macaroni & cheese	4x	$0.39
lunch meat	1x	$0.99
hot dogs (fat free)	1x	$0.99
mozzarella, 8 oz.	1x	$1.09
chocolate chips	1x	$0.99
kidney beans, can	2x	$0.49
tuna	2x	$0.49
canned tomatoes	2x	$0.69
elbow macaroni	2x	$0.50
cream cheese (lowfat)	1x	$0.99
cold boxed cereal	2x	$1.99
peanut butter	1x	$1.50
Total		$28.35

Grocery Store #3	unit cost	
spaghetti sauce	2x	$0.99
spinach, can 16 oz.	1x	$0.89
potatoes, 10 lb. bag	1x	$0.99
pork roast ($0.79/lb)	5x	$0.79
margarine	2x	$0.50
ground turkey	3x	$0.89
lettuce	5x	$0.59
popcorn, kernels	1x	$0.79
yams	3x	$0.33
cottage cheese, 16 oz.		$1.29
chicken legs	4x	$0.49
tomato sauce, 8 oz.	1x	$0.49
chicken broth, instant	1x	$1.29
onion	3x	$0.20
pineapple, chunks, can	1x	$0.69
raisins	1x	$2.89
leeks	2x	$0.50
garlic, bunch	1x	$0.35
tomatoes	1 lb.	$0.79
carrots	2 lb.	$0.79
bell pepper	1x	$0.39
zucchini	4 lb.	$0.79
hamburger buns	1x	$0.69
lasagna noodles	1x	$0.50
Total		$37.45

Trader Joe's	unit cost	
milk	8x	$1.99
tofu	2x	$0.88
bagels	1x	$0.99
cheese (4 lbs. @ $1.99/lb)		$7.96
Total		$26.63

Appendix A

Warehouse Store		unit cost
fruit, in season, 10 lb.	1x	$3.89
canned tomatoes (6)	1x	$3.00
chicken breasts (4 lbs.)	2x	$9.58
frozen juice (6)	1x	$5.89
sliced ham lunch meat	1x	$5.89
Total		$41.22

MONTHLY TOTAL	**$153.53**
AVERAGE WEEKLY TOTAL	**$38.38**

Substitutions, Equivalency Tables, and Metric Conversion

SUBSTITUTIONS

Dairy

3 oz. cream cheese	= 6 T. cream cheese
1 cup crumbled blue cheese	= 4 oz. blue cheese
1-1/4 cups grated cheese	= 1/4 pound hard cheese
1 cup shredded hard cheese (Cheddar, Swiss)	= 4 ounces cheese
1-1/4 cup shredded soft cheese (Monterey Jack, American)	= 4 oz. cheese
2 cups whipped cream	= 1 cup heavy cream before beating
1 whole egg	= 2 egg yolks
1 cup of sour milk	= 1 T. lemon juice or vinegar plus 1 cup milk
1 cup buttermilk	= 1 cup yogurt

Chocolate

3 T. dry cocoa plus 1 T. butter	= 1 square unsweetened chocolate
1 square	= 1 ounce
1 square	= 4 T. grated chocolate
1 pound cocoa	= 4 cups

Nuts

1 pound almonds in shells	= 1-1/4 cups almond meat
1 pound pecans in shells	= 2-1/4 cups chopped pecans
1 pound walnut in shells	= 1-1/2 cups walnut meat
1 pound peanuts in shells	= 2-1/4 cups peanuts

Pasta and Breads

1 cup uncooked rice	= 3 cups cooked rice
1/4 pound uncooked pasta	= 2 cups cooked pasta
Make 1 C. of fine crumbs with	= 4 slices bread
or	= 28 unsalted crackers
or	= 14 graham crackers squares
bread crumbs	= dry pancake mix when desperate
1 cup bread cubes	= 2 slices bread
1 pound oats	= 2–2/3 cups
Pie crust	= line pan with mashed canned beans, mashed potatoes, cooked rice or noodles

Baking/Spices

1 tsp. baking powder	= 1/4 tsp. baking soda + 1/2 tsp. cream of tartar
1 cup cake flour	= 1 cup all-purpose flour + 2 T. cornstarch
1 cup self-rising flour	= 1 cup flour + 1–1/2 tsp. baking powder + 1/2 tsp. salt
2 cups corn syrup	= 1 cup sugar
1 cup honey	= 1–1/4 cup sugar
1 cup molasses	= 3/4 cup sugar
1–1/4 cups confectioners sugar	= 1 cup granulated sugar
1 T. instant minced onion rehydrated	= 1 small fresh onion
1 T. prepared mustard	= 1 tsp. mustard
1/8 tsp. garlic powder	= 1 small clove garlic
2 T. of flour	= 1 T. cornstarch to use as a thickening agent
Ketchup or chili	= 1 cup tomato sauce plus 1/2 cup sugar and 2 T. vinegar
1 tsp. dried herbs	= 1 T. fresh herbs
1 pkg. [2 teaspoons] active dry yeast	= 1 cake compressed yeast
1 pound box of these sugars	= 2 cups white sugar
or	= 2–1/4 cup brown sugar
or	= 3–1/2 cups confectioners sugar
2 cups butter	= 1 lb.
8–10 egg whites	= 1 cup
12–14 yolks	= 1 cup

Fruits

1 large apple	= 1 cup sliced apple
3 bananas	= 1-1/2 cups mashed bananas
	or 2 cups sliced bananas
1 lemon	= 2–3 T. lemon juice
1 lime	= 1–2 T. lime juice
1 quart berries	= 3-1/2 cups
1 pound dried apricots	= 3 cups
1 pound raisins	= 2-3/4 cup

Vegetables and Legumes

1 cup chopped celery	= 2 stalks celery
1/2 cup chopped onion	= 1 medium sized onion
3 potatoes	= 1-1/4 cup mashed potato
1 pound raw potatoes	= 2 cups mashed potatoes
1 pound dried beans	= 6–9 cups cooked
1 cup canned tomatoes	= 1-1/3 cup cut up fresh tomatoes
1 lb. fresh tomatoes	= 1-1/2 cups chopped

EQUIVALENCIES TABLE

dash	= less than 1/8 tsp.
3 tsp.	= 1 T.
4 T.	= 1/4 cup
8 T.	= 1/2 cup
8 T.	= 4 ounces
16 T.	= 1 cup
7/8 cup	= 3/4 cup + 2 T.
1 T.	= 1/2 fluid ounce
8 oz. can or jar	= 1 cup
10 1/2 oz. can	= 1-1/4 cup
12 oz. tuna can	= 1-1/2 cup
2-1/2 lb. can	= 3-1/2 cup
15 oz. can	= 1-1/3 cups
8 quarts (dry)	= 1 peck
4 pecks	= 1 bushel
16 ounces (dry)	= 1 pound

METRIC CONVERSION CHART

1 gram	= .035 ounces
1 kilogram	= 2.21 pounds
1 ounce	= 29 grams
1 tsp.	= 5 milliliters
1 T.	= 15 milliliters
1 cup	= 237 milliliters
1 pound	= 454 grams
1 liter	= 1.056 liquid quarts or 1000 milliliters
1 quart	= 0.946 liters

COST BREAKDOWNS

(based on sale prices)

1 cup flour	= 5¢
1 egg	= 9¢
1/2 cup butter	= 25¢
1 apple	= 7¢

Resources

HERE ARE SOME VERY GOOD additional resources for learning more about how to live on less, cooking inexpensively, creating a budget, building a savings account, improving the safety and healthfulness of your home, starting a home business, cutting your utility bills, and teaching your children about money.

BOOKS

Books On Miserly Living

Babbitt, Dave and Kathy. *Downscaling: Simplify & Enrich Your Lifestyle,* Moody Press, 1993

Bowman, Linda. *Free Food & More,* Probus Publishing Company, 1991

Bowman, Linda. *Free Stuff For Your Pet,* Probus Publishing Company, 1991

Brennen, Sherri. *Better Living—Tips For Saving Time and Money,* WVEC-TV Inc., 1994

Burkett, Larry. *Women Leaving The Workplace,* Moody Press, 1995

Dacyczyn, Amy. *The Tightwad Gazette,* Villard Books, 1993

Dacyczyn, Amy. *The Tightwad Gazette II,* Villard Books, 1995

Dappen, Andy. *Cheap Tricks—100s Of Ways You Can Save 1000s of Dollars,* Brier Books, 1992

Editors of Rodale. *Cut Your Bills In Half,* Rodale Press, 1989

Editors of Rodale. *Cut Your Spending In Half Without Settling For Less,* Rodale Press 1994

Fields, Denise and Alan. *Baby Bargains,* Windsor Peak Press, 1995

Gallagher, Patricia. *Raising Happy Kids On A Reasonable Budget,* Better Way Books, 1993

Gorman, Charlotte. *The Frugal Mind—1,479 Money Saving Tips For Surviving The 1990s,* Nottingham Books, 1990

Hardy, Dawn. *Bargains-By-Mail For Baby And You,* Prima Publishing, 1992

Hatton, Hap and Torbet, Laura. *Helpful Hints For Better Living—How To Live Better For Less,* Facts On File Publication, 1984

Hatton, Hap and Torbet, Laura. *Helpful Hints For Hard Times: How To Live It Up While Cutting Down,* Facts On File Publication, 1983

Hunt, Mary. *The Best Of The Cheapskate Monthly—Simple Tips For Living Lean In The 90s,* St. Martin's Paperbacks, 1993

Kenyon, Mary. *Home Schooling From Scratch,* Gazelle Publications, 1996

King, Dean. *Penny Pinchers Almanac—Handbook For Modern Frugality,* Simon & Schuster, 1992

Kunes, Ellen. *Living Well Or Even Better On Less,* Byron Preiss Visual Publication, 1991

Lederman, Ellen. *Making Life More Livable,* Fireside Book, 1994

Lesko, Matthew. *1,001 Free Goodies & Cheapies,* Information USA, Inc. 1994

Luck, Kenny. *52 Ways To Stretch A Buck,* Thomas Nelson Publishers, 1992

McDonald, Rochette L. *How To Pinch A Penny Till It Screams,* Avery Publishing, 1994

Moore, Ron and Melodie. *Smart Cents,* Stern Sloan, 1993

Nader, Ralph and Smith, Wesley J. *The Frugal Shopper,* Center For Study Of Responsive Law, 1992

Pond, Jonathan D. *1001 Ways To Cut Your Expenses,* Dell Publishing, 1992

Roberts, William. *How To Save Money On Just About Everything,* Strebor Publications, 1993

Roth, Larry. *The Best of Living Cheap News,* Contemporary Books, 1996

Sanders, Darcie and Bullen, Martha M. *Never Throw Out A Banana Again And 364 Other Ways To Save Money At Home,* Crown Trade Paperbacks, 1995

Simmons, Lee and Barbara. *Penny Pinching—How To Lower Your Everyday Expenses Without Lowering Your Standard Of Living,* Bantam Books, 1991

Soreuson, Stephen and Amanda. *Living Smart, Spending Less,* Moody Press, 1993

Yorkey, Mike. *Saving Money Anyway You Can,* Vine Books, 1994

Books On Grocery Savings & Cooking Inexpensive Meals

Barfield, Rhonda. *Eat Well For $50 A Week,* Lilac Publishing, 1993

Birnes, Nancy. *Cheaper & Better—Homemade Alternatives To Store Brought Goods,* Harper & Row Publishers, 1988

Bond, Jill. *Dinner's In The Freezer!—More Mary And Less Martha,* GCB Publishing, 1993

Dojny, Brooke. *Cheap Eats: Simple, Sumptuous Meals For Four You Can Make,* Harper Perennial, 1993

Edwards, Pat. *Cheap Eating—How to Feed Your Family Well And Spend Less,* Upper Access Books, 1993

Hartwig, Daphne. *Make Your Own Groceries,* Bobbs-Merrill, 1983

Hillson, Cynthia. *Thriving On Thrift—A Common Sense Guide To Feeding Your Family For Less,* Thriving On Thrift Publishing, 1995

Hood, Joan. *Will It Freeze—An A To Z Guide To Foods That Freeze,* Charles Scribner's Sons, 1982

Longacre, Doris J. *More-With-Less Cookbook,* Herald Press, 1986

Rothman, Marcie. *The $5.00 Chef—How To Save Cash & Cook Fast,* Five-Spot Press, 1991

Salsbury, Barbara. *Cut Your Grocery Bills In Half!,* Acropolis Books, 1982

Speigel, Janet. *Stretching The Food Dollar,* Chronicle Books, 1981

Willand, Lois C. *The Use-It-Up Cookbook—A Guide for Minimizing Food Waste,* Practical Cookbooks, 1979

Wilson, Mimi and Lagerborg, Mary Beth. *Once-A-Month Cooking,* Focus On The Family, 1986

Witty, Elizabeth and Colchie, Elizabeth. *Better Than Store-Bought,* Perennial Library, 1979

Books On Family Budgeting And Savings

Blue, Ron. *Master Your Money,* Thomas Nelson Publishers, 1991

Briles, Judith. *Moneysense—What Every Women Must Know To Be Financially Confident,* Moody Press, 1995

Burkett, Larry. *The Complete Financial Guide For Single Parents,* Victor Press, 1992

Burkett, Larry. *Using Your Money Wisely,* Moody Press, 1990

Burkett, Larry. *Your Finances In Changing Times,* Moody Press, 1993

Humber, Wilson J. *Dollars & Sense—Making The Most Of What You Have,* Navpress, 1993

Matthews, Micheal. *The Little Book Money Clips,* Multhomah Books, 1994

Moe, Harold. *Make Your Paycheck Last,* Career Press, 1993

O' Neill, Barbara. *Saving On A Shoestring—How To Cut Expenses, Reduce debt, Stash More Cash,* Dearborn Financial Publishing Inc., 1995

Pond, Jonathan. *The New Century Family Money Book,* Dell Hardcover, 1993

Savage, Terry. *Terry Savage's New Money: Strategies For The 90's,* Harper Business, 1994

Scott, David. *The Guide To Personal Budgeting—How To Stretch Your Dollars Through Wise Money Management,* A Globe Pequot, 1995

Wall, Ginita. *The Way To Save: A 10-Step Blueprint For Lifetime Security,* Henry Holt and Co., 1993

Books On Getting Out of Debt
& Being Financially Free

Blue, Ron. *Taming The Money Monster—Five Steps To Conquering Debt,* Focus On The Family Publishing, 1993

Brunette, William K. *Conquer Your Debt,* Prentice Hall Press, 1990

Burkett, Larry. *Debt-Free Living: How To Get Out Of Debt & Stay Out,* Moody Press, 1989

Feinberg, Andrew. *Down Size Your Debt,* Penguin Books, 1993

Hammond, Bob. *Life After Debt: How To Repair Your Credit And Get Out Of Debt Once And For All,* Career Press, 1993

Hunt, Mary. *The Cheapskate Monthly Money Makeover,* St. Martin's Paperbacks, 1995

Mundis, Jerrold. *How to Get Out Of Debt, Stay Out Of Debt & Live Prosperously,* Bantam Books, 1990

Paris, James L. *Living Financially Free,* Harvest House Publishers, 1994

Thomsett, Michael C. *How To Get Out Of Debt,* Irwin Publishing, 1990

Books On Safe & Healthy Households

Berthold-Bond, Annie. *Clean & Green: The Complete Guide To Non-Toxic Environmentally Safe Housekeeps,* Ceres Press, 1990

Bower, Lynn M. *The Healthy Household—A Complete Guide For Creating A Healthy Indoor Environment,* The Healthy House Institute, 1995

Dadd, Debra L. *Nontoxic, Natural & Earthwise,* Jeremy P. Tarcher/Perigee, 1990

Hayes, Alan B. *Reclaim, Recycle, Reuse All Natural Products To Help Save The Earth,* Sally Milner Publishing, 1992

Hunter, Linda M. *The Healthy Home: An Attic-To-Basement Guide To Toxin-Free Living,* Rodale Press, 1989

Lifton, Bernice. *Bug Busters—Poison-Free Pest Controls For Your House & Garden,* Avery Publishing, 1991

Rinzler, Carol A. *The Consumer's Brand—Name Guide To Household Products,* Lippincott & Crowell Publishers, 1980

Stevens, Chris. *Helpful Household Hints: A Consumers Guide To Making Life Easier & Safer Around Your Home,* Brown Publishing, 1991

Books On Starting a Home Business

Arden, Lynie. *The Work-At-Home Source Book,* Live Oak Publishing, 1994

Brabec, Barbara. *Homemade Money—How To Select, Start, Manage, Market And Multiply The Profits Of A Business At Home,* Better Way Books, 1994

Edwards, Paul and Sarah. *The Best Home Businesses For The 90s,* G. P. Putnam's Sons, 1991

Edwards, Paul and Sarah. *Working From Home,* G. P. Putnam's Sons, 1994

Elyer, David R. *The Home Business Bible,* John Wiley & Sons, 1994

Glenn, Reed. *Ten Best Opportunities For Starting A Home Business Today,* Live Oak Publications, 1993

Hanania, David. *Home Business Made Easy,* Oasis Press, 1992

Hicks, Tyler G. *199 Great Home Businesses You Can Start And Succeed In For Under $1,000,* Prima Publishing, 1993

Huff, Priscilla Y. *101 Best Home-Based Businesses For Women,* Prima Publishing, 1995

Levinson, Jay. *550 Ways To Earn Extra Money,* Henry Holt, 1991

Partow, Donna. *Homemade Business—A Woman's Step-By-Step Guide To Earning Money At Home,* Focus on the Family Publishing, 1992

Books On The Perspective of Staying Home With Your Children

Davidson, Christine. *Staying Home Instead: Alternatives To The Two-Paycheck Family,* Macmillan, 1993

Field, Christine. *Coming Home To Raise Your Children—A Survival Guide For Moms,* Revell, 1995

Hunter, Brenda. *Home By Choice: A Decision Every Mother Must Face,* Multnomah Books, 1993

McHugh, Jennifer and DeSena, Jeannie. *The Best Of The Proverbs 31 Homemaker—Encouragement And Ideas For Wives and Mothers,* Proverbs 31 Homemaker Press, 1996

Sanders, Darcie and Bullen, Martha. *Staying Home: From Full-time Professional To Full-Time Parent,* Little, Brown and Co., 1992

Tolliver, Cindy. *At-Home Motherhood—Making It Work For You,* Resource Publication, 1994

Books On Cutting Your Utility Bills

Albright, Roger. *547 Easy Ways To Save Energy In Your Home,* Garden Way Publishing, 1978

Herbert, Ralph J. *Cut Your Electric Bills In Half,* Rodale Press, 1989

Laird Jean E. *Homemaker's Book Of Energy Savers,* Macmillian, 1982

Wilson, Alex. *Consumer Guide To Home Energy Savings,* American Council For An Energy-Efficient Economy, 1990

Books On Cutting Medical & Insurance Bills

Nader, Ralph and Smith, Wesley J. *Winning The Insurance Game,* Doubleday, 1993

Ulene, Art. *How To Cut Your Medical Bills,* Ulysses Press, 1994

Books On Kids, Crafts & Inexpensive Family Fun

Bennett, Steve and Ruth. *Cabin Fever,* Penguin Books, 1994

Bowman, Linda. *Freebies For Kids & Parents Too!,* Probus Publishing Company, 1991

Dondiego, Barbara L. *Crafts For Kids—A Month-By-Month Idea Book,* Tab Books, 1991

Dunne, Margaret. *Children's Party Ideas,* Berkley Books, 1994

Krautwurst, Gwen and Terry. *Nature Crafts For Kids—50 Fantastic Things To Make With Mother Nature's Help,* Sterling Publishing Co., 1992

Keeshan, Bob. *Family Fun Activity Book,* Deaconess Press, 1995

Macgregor, Cynthia. *Free Family Fun And Super Cheap,* Berkley Books, 1994

Macgregor, Cynthia. *Mommy, There's Nothing To Do!,* Berkley Books, 1993

Marzollo, Jean. *Birthday Parties For Children: How To Give Them, How To Survive Them,* Perennial Library, 1983

Treinen, Sara J. *Incredibly Awesome Crafts For Kids,* Better Homes And Gardens Books, 1992

Books On Money And Kids

Berg, Adriane G. *The Totally Awesome Money Book For Kids And Their Parents,* Prentice-Hall, 1993

Blue, Ron and Judy. *Raising Money-Smart Kids—How To Teach Your Children The Secrets Of Earning, Saving, Investing, And Spending Wisely,* Thomas Nelson Publishers, 1992

Bodnar, Janet. *Money Smart Kids,* Kiplinger Books, 1993

NEWSLETTER DIRECTORY

If the sample copy of any newsletter is free, please include a self-addressed stamped envelope with your request.

Larry Roth
LIVING CHEAP NEWS
7232 Belleview Avenue
Kansas City, MO 64114
(816) 523-3161
$12/yr/10 issues
Sample copy: $1.00 with #10 SASE

Cynthia Hillson
THRIVING ON THRIFT
   P.O. Box 2036
   Cornelius, NC 28031
   (704) 664-7971
   $12 /yr/4 issues
   Sample copy: $1.00

Mary Hunt
THE CHEAPSKATE MONTHLY
   P.O. Box 2135
   Paramount, CA 90723-8135
   (310) 630-8845
   $15.95/yr/12 issues
   Sample copy: Free with #10 SASE

Diane Rosener
A PENNY SAVED
   P.O. Box 3471
   Omaha, NE 68103-0471
   $15.00/yr/10 issues
   Sample copy: $2.00

Patti Anderson
FROZEN ASSETS
   6005 North 116 Plaza
   Omaha, NE 68164-1429
   $12/yr/12 issues
   Sample copy: Free with #10 SASE

Tracey McBride
FRUGAL TIMES: MAKING DO WITH DIGNITY
   P.O. Box 5877
   Garden Grove, CA 92645
   $12/yr/8 issues
   Sample copy: $1.00

Edith Kilgo
CREATIVE DOWNSCALING
P.O. Box 1884, Dept. MM
Jonesboro, GA 30237-1884
(770) 471-9048
$16.00/yr/10 issues
Sample copy: $2.00

Robert Frank
NO-DEBT LIVING
P.O. Box 282
Veradale, WA 99037
(800) 560-3328
$25.95/yr/11 issues
Sample copy: $2.00

Ron and Melodie Moore
TIGHTWAD LIVING
P.O. Box 818
Palm Harbor, FL 34682
(813) 785-7759
$12.00/yr/12 issues
Sample copy: $2.95

Leslie Maupin
POOR RICHARD'S ALMANAC II
3317 South Southlyn Place
Springfield, MO 65804-6435
(417) 887-4212
$12/yr/12 issues
Sample copy: $1.00 with #10 SASE

Marc Eisenson
THE POCKET CHANGE INVESTOR
P.O. Box 78
Elizaville, NY 12523
(914) 758-1400
$12.95/yr/4 issues
Sample copy: $1.00

Pat Wesolowski
BIG IDEAS SMALL BUDGET
    2201 High Road
    Tallahassee, FL 32303
    (904) 385-1958
    $12/yr/11 issues
    Sample copy: $1.00

Rick Doble
SAVVY DISCOUNTS NEWSLETTER
    PO Box 96
    Smyrna, NC 28579
    (800) 308-1901
    $14.95/yr/4 issues
    Sample copy: Free with #10 SASE

Jennifer Mchugh
THE PROVERBS 31 HOMEMAKER
    P.O. Box 17155
    Charlotte, NC 28270
    (704) 849-2270
    $15/yr/12 issues
    Sample copy: $1.00

Stephana Burkett
PROSPERITY GAZETTE
    RR 1, P.O. Box 566
    Big Sandy, TX 75755-9650
    $15/yr/12 issues
    Sample copy: $1.00 with #10 SASE

Susan Gregory
OUT OF THE RAT RACE
    P.O. Box 95341
    Seattle, WA 98145
    (206) 524-9400
    $12/yr/10 issues
    Sample copy: Free with #10 SASE

Cindy VanGelder
KEEP YOUR CASH
> P.O. Box 2234
> Holland, MI 49422
> $12.00/yr/12 issues
> Sample copy: Free with SASE

Roy and Lorraine Maxsons
THE CHEAP REPORT
> P.O. Box 394
> Antioch, CA 94509
> (510) 779-9329
> $12.00/yr/10 issues
> Sample copy: $1.10

Lowell and Deborah Tukua
COMING HOME MAGAZINE
> P.O. Box 367
> Savannah, TN 38372-0367
> (615) 724-5493
> $18.00/yr/6 issues (60 pages each issue)
> Sample copy: $3.00

Mark Miller
SENSIBLE SAVER
> 6488 Victory Dr.
> Acworth, GA 30102
> (800) 231-1994
> $24.95/yr/12 issues
> Sample copy: $3.00

Notes

INDEX